Ride Free
From Fear to Fun

Release Your Fears,
Reconnect to Your Horse,
and Ride with Confidence

Second Edition

Written by Miranda K. Velasquez

Copyright

Printed in the United States of America
Second printing, 2019

Originally published under the title, "Riding
Scared: A Spiritual Guide to Connecting with
Yourself and Your Horse"

Cover Design by: Miranda K. Velasquez
Book Design and Production by: Miranda K.
Velasquez
Editing by: Sarah Jenkinson

Disclaimer

The information in this book is meant to supplement, not replace, proper equestrian training. Like any sport involving animals, speed, equipment, balance and environmental factors, horse-riding poses some inherent risk. The author and publisher advise readers to take full responsibility for their safety and know their limits. Before practicing the skills described in this book, be sure that your equipment is well maintained, you and your horse are properly trained, and do not take risks beyond your level of experience, aptitude, training, or comfort.

The exercises laid out in this book are similar to those recommended by licensed counselors. Following them can help manage anxiety and fears, both when mounted or not. However, for those who have more advanced physical disabilities or mental health disorders, this book does not replace the need for professional help. Please, if you have disabilities that prevent you from riding without assistance, find a licensed professional that can help you. Your safety is most important.

Dedication

This book is dedicated to my beautiful mare, Paris, who has been by my side through all of life's pleasures and pains, and to my magnificent little family: David, Remy, Elleni, Andalynn, and Weston. I appreciate your love and support, both while writing this book and throughout all of life.

To David, my loving and supportive spouse, you have given me the wings to fly and I am forever grateful.

To my children, I only hope that you will one day see that you are my reason for everything I do. You give me the reason to have courage, be strong, and step out of the shadows. My only wish for you all is that you achieve your dreams, no matter what they may be.

Table of Contents

Disclaimer 3
Dedication 4

Chapter 1: Ride Free 10
~ Wisdom from Paris . . . 22

Chapter 2: Who Am I and Why Do I Want to Help You? 24
~ Wisdom from Paris . . . 43

Chapter 3: My 10-Step Solution for Releasing Your Fears 44
~ Wisdom from Paris . . . 57

Chapter 4: Could It Be Me? 59
~ Exercise 1: Weighing the Positives and Negatives . . . 62
~ Exercise 2: Weekly Joy Thoughts . . . 65
~ Exercise 3: Pinpointing Your Negative Patterns . . . 70

~ Barn Action . . . 72

~ Wisdom from Paris . . . 75

Chapter 5: Opening To Forgiveness 76

~ Exercise 4: Releasing Your Emotions . . . 77

~ Exercise 5: Finding Forgiveness . . . 82

~ Barn Action . . . 91

~ Wisdom from Paris . . . 92

Chapter 6: Never Letting Fear Win 94

~ Exercise 6: Understanding Your
                    Emotions . . . 102

~ Barn Action . . . 106

~ Wisdom from Paris . . . 107

Chapter 7: Nailing a Positive Mindset 109

~ Exercise 7: Mastering Your Mindset . . . 113

~ Wisdom from Paris . . . 122

**Chapter 8: Embracing Love, Healing Energy,
and Magic 124**

~ Exercise 8: Accessing Your Wounded Inner
Child . . . 131

~ Exercise 9: The Releasing Bubble
Meditation . . . 134

~ The Animal as Healing Helper . . . 137

~ Exercise 10: The Heart Map . . . 139

~ Barn Action . . . 141

~ Wisdom from Paris . . . 142

**Chapter 9: Counting On Your Intuitive
Confidence 143**

~ Exercise 11: Mirror Work . . . 146

~ Intuition . . . 149

~ Wisdom from Paris . . . 154

**Chapter 10: Trusting the Divine and Finding
Your Balance 155**

~ Balance . . . 155

~ Spirituality . . . 159

~ The Horse-Human Connection . . . 161

~ Exercise 12: Studying Your Horse's
Behavior . . . 164

~ Wisdom from Paris . . . 166

Chapter 11: Is Your Relationship with Your Horse Strong Enough? 167
~ Barn Action . . . 178
~ Wisdom from Paris . . . 179

Chapter 12: Notes for Those with Disabilities, Competitive Riders, and How to Connect with Other People's Horses 180
~Disabilities . . . 180
~Competing on Your Horse or Someone
    Else's . . . 184
~ Barn Action . . . 194
~ Wisdom from Paris . . . 195

Chapter 13: Giving Up is NOT an Option 196
~ Wisdom from Paris . . . 206

About the Author 208

Chapter 1: Ride Free

"If you are fearful, a horse will back off. If you are calm and confident, it will come forward. For those who are often flattered or feared, the horse can be a welcome mirror of the best in human nature."

~Clare Balding

When you dreamed of riding horses, what did you envision? I imagine that you pictured yourself riding beautifully with the wind in your hair, feeling the greatest connection between you and your horse, and having so much fun!

Maybe you have had horses all your life and you just always knew they were going to play a big role in it. Somehow, even though you grew up with them, you couldn't explain the feeling you had when you were with them. It was a feeling of peace, love, and acceptance.

But no matter *when* horses appeared in your life–or if they haven't yet made their appearance and you're still waiting patiently for your turn with the majestic beasts–they have always made an impression on you. They have made you desire to be with them. They've called out and touched the deepest part of your soul, and all you can hope for is to have that beautiful connection you both long so deeply for.

When you finally got your first horse, I bet you were the happiest person in the world. It doesn't matter how old you were, whether you were a child or an adult, the excitement and love you felt could not be matched.

Do you remember those tender touches, nose to nose, a new relationship just beginning? It was sweet and special, a connection between you and your horse that no one else could touch, always together in each other's hearts.

You may have had dreams of competing in the Olympics or winning a barrel event at the local rodeo. You may have even achieved those dreams until it happened.

You had great rides, won competitions, trained well, had fun, and rode fearlessly. You met friends, camped, had a few falls, had more great rides, loved that horse like no one else could, and he loved you, too! You were best friends, two peas in a pod, couldn't be separated, and then something changed.

What changed? Why did it change? Where did the connection go? That deep longing to be together faded. Maybe you know why it faded, maybe you don't, but the connection has been lost. The fear has set in, and you cannot ride your horse without the shadows creeping in from your mind.

You went from riding all the time to having a pasture ornament, and now you're feeling low, angry, guilty, and ashamed. I know it doesn't make you feel good to see your horse sitting out in your pasture not being ridden. Or even worse, paying the board for your non-ridden horse at a facility, am I right?

Are you tired of being scared to ride? Are you tired of riding scared? You know: clenching every muscle in your body because your horse popped his head up. Or if he shakes while you're on, your heart starts pumping a million beats a minute because you thought for sure you were going to get dumped again.

Those reactions are normal for someone who is afraid to get injured. If you've had a bad fall you may be feeling less than enthusiastic about getting on the back of that horse at all. (Don't worry, we go over how to just BE with your horse in Chapter 11, in case you really don't think you can ever ride again, or you just want to redefine your relationship with your horse.)

Now, before we get into the reconnection techniques I'll describe in this book, let's talk about safety. It's important to address what things this book *does* cover, and what it *doesn't*.

First and foremost, if you are afraid of your horse–afraid to handle your horse, or even to touch your horse–then please be safe and have someone else assist you who is NOT afraid of your horse. Someone who can handle your horse and help you to stay safe.

This is extremely important. If you don't currently feel safe and confident being near your horse, you need to have a handler present so that all future interactions with your horse are positive. Horses remember and differentiate between positive and negative interactions, so it's important that you make sure you're only reinforcing positivity with them.

Remember: the most important part of this equation is your safety and wellbeing. Horses can be mischievous, unpredictable, and spook easily. If you are unskilled or afraid to handle your horse, please NEVER handle them alone.

Secondly, if you have a horse that is young and untrained, or if you are not *already* a skilled horse handler, you will need more than what this book offers. Before you begin implementing any of the tools and strategies I describe in this book, you should know, at minimum, how to halter and lead your horse safely.

I emphasize this because I want you to keep yourself safe. If you are unsure whether you're skilled enough, please hire or find someone to help you before you do anything else.

This book does not replace foundational training for either horse or rider, it does not recommend training techniques for your horse, and it does not recommend or reprimand your use of a helmet. What it *does* do is help you replace your fears with confidence after you've either lost confidence with your horse, or never had that confidence to begin with.

Maybe you had a fall. Maybe you watched a friend fall. Maybe your horse was injured and you're afraid to re-injure him again. No matter the reason, the fears are there in the corner of your mind, holding you back from accomplishing your goals.

Goals? You may think I'm crazy to even bring up goals in the first chapter of this book, because at this point, you'd be happy to just look at your horse without fear or guilt. How can you even think about goals?!

I assure you, goals are still there, waiting to be resurrected once your confidence is regained. The fear may be there at the moment, preventing you from doing what you love to do, and what you want to do. But it's when you dare to dream of riding again that you find those goals speaking to you.

Even when the fear rushes in and you dismiss those dreams just as quickly as they appeared, they are still there, waiting patiently for you to find your way back to your horse. They are your horse dreams yet to be realized, but still circling close to the surface, waiting for your fears to subside enough that you will dare to dream again.

If your goal is to reconnect with your horse or get back in the saddle, then I wrote this book for you. The techniques outlined within will help you to uncover your fears at their deepest level so that you can release them, heal them, and move forward to whatever goal you may have.

Are you looking to compete at high-level dressage events, the NFR, the local gymkhana, or the American Royal? Maybe your goal is just to get back on your backyard horse and feel comfortable at the trot. Do you want to just reconnect with your horse? Feel free to love him without fear clouding your every move? Throw your arms around his neck and let him hug you back? Walk him down the road without the fear that he's going to jump on you when a bird rustles the bush?

There are so many scenarios and all of them can become reality when you learn the steps to release your fears, commit to confidence, and embrace your soul. These lessons can apply to all areas of your life and all fears. Embrace these lessons, use them, and remember them; they will be with you forever.

The biggest part of this journey is going to be allowing yourself to really feel UNcomfortable, swing wide, and make that deep change. You may be thinking, "Why do I need to change?" Or, "I really won't change that much. I'll just get past my fears and go back to being the same old me." But if you're reading this book then I can tell that you don't want to be the same old you.

Just by picking up this book you've taken the first step to understanding yourself. You have gone further than many other people will ever go in beating their fears and you've stated very loudly that you love your horse and yourself enough to fix your problem.

What is that problem? The very general problem that everyone who reads this book will have is that fear is getting the best of them and they don't like it. You will know your very specialized and specific fear by the time you are done working through this book, plus have a plan in place for how to fix it as well. Then it will be up to you to decide on whether you continue to work to fix your problem or not.

Here is something that I can say with absolute certainty: if you don't do the work to fix your problem, you will go back to being the same old you, and that's NOT what you want. You may want to keep some parts of yourself the same, but I'm sure you'd love a few pieces of you to change as well.

Just because it SEEMS comfortable where you are right now, is it really? It probably isn't as comfortable as you'd like to think it is. Think about it: is it really comfortable to continue in your routine of fear, no confidence, and completely judging yourself? Is that what you call happiness and comfort? Judging yourself, feeling guilty, being disconnected from your horse, and thinking you can't do it?

Wouldn't you prefer to feel like you can do anything, be able to accept yourself for who you are, become deeply connected with your horse again, and feel full of love? Which sounds like the better way of being, living, and thinking? The "loving and living life to its fullest" option or the "feeling disconnected from your horse, other people, and life in general" option?

So now do you understand why you NEED to change? Not all parts of you will change, but hopefully your mindset and your fears will. It's up to you just how much you want to change or how little.

Oh, and by the way, if you think you've gotten to this point in your life without change, that's unheard of. We all have to change or we don't grow. How can you become an equestrian or even just a backyard horse rider without change? You have to learn, adapt, and grow.

Maybe that's what your true fear is: your ability to change with your horse. Are you afraid that your horse is better than you, or maybe too good for you? Maybe you're too green of a rider for your more accomplished horse?

I know I went through that stage myself. I was a green rider with a green horse and I was sure as sure could be that something needed to change. I thought we couldn't figure it out together; one of us had to know more to teach the other. Well, the Universe slapped me in the face by having us learn everything together, and quickly, too.

Let me state this in very clear terms for you: there is nothing you can't overcome when you put fear aside, embrace change, and change your mind to reflect that you CAN do this. You'll feel the difference and your horse will, too. Does that mean you'll be competing next week? Probably not, but with time it's possible...if you're willing, and dedicated to working through and releasing your fears.

A very smart woman once said, "You can't get the results if you don't do the work." Are you willing to do the work? This might seem really early in the book to start discussing "the work," but I know horse owners. You want results fast and don't have time to sit and ponder, so here I am getting real with you.

This is why I also want you to consider using a journal while you work through this book. Journaling is very cathartic and can help you to recognize patterns, accept them, and change them. This may not be easy to do for some, and for others it may feel great. It really will depend on the amount of effort you choose to put into your relationship with your horse.

So, stop reading right now and make the decision. I really want you to think about this. Are you willing to dedicate the time and energy that is required to get back on that horse? Are you willing to dig deep, be uncomfortable, and change who you are and what you believe at your core? That's usually what happens; when you change and shift, you feel differently, and act differently...and eventually you live differently because you are no longer living in fear.

It can be really magical and an epic journey if you're open and willing to dedicate the time and do the work. If you're not ready right now, set the book down and come back when you are. There is no shame in admitting that you're not ready. In fact, it's an important step in realizing just who you are and what you're capable of. If you *are* ready, keep reading and let's get this epic, magical journey of change underway.

Once again, I encourage you to incorporate journaling into this work. You are welcome to simply journal about your thoughts or feelings as you do the exercises outlined in each chapter, but there's another option available, as well.

I have created a specific set of journaling prompts that correlate with the work you will be doing in each chapter. These prompts were created to make it easier for you to process your fears, and get back on your horse that much quicker. I will share more about these prompts with you at the end of Chapter 3, so that you're ready to begin using them in Chapter 4, where the real work starts.

Wisdom From Paris

The other day a storm was rolling in and I got really scared. I reared, jumped and bucked on a walk with my mom. I'm not sure what scared me so much, but I've never acted like that before. What made it a great day was that my mom reacted in a safe way. She didn't let go of my lead rope, and she didn't get scared. She stayed with me. She stroked my neck and said some nice words really quietly to me. I really liked that.

I wanted to go back to my stall where I knew I was safe, but my mom didn't let me go right away. That made me a little upset, and I went crazy again. She understood what I wanted, but she also knew that I needed to see there wasn't anything scary that was going to eat me. After a few minutes, we walked back to my stall and she made shushing noises while I looked at everything. You know what...I didn't get eaten! I am so grateful my mom took the time to help me. She really loves me.

Chapter 2: Who Am I and Why Do I Want to Help You?

"Some horses will test you, some will teach you, and some will bring out the best in you."

~Unknown

You may be wondering who I am and why I am here, offering my help to you. Maybe you're wondering how I know the things that I know and do the things that I do. Well, that's quite a long story, but I'm going to share it with you.

On September 30th of 2010, I lost my mom to breast cancer at age 59. This was quickly followed by a divorce from my husband of 10 years and my stepdad, who I am very close to, being diagnosed with Stage 3 colon cancer in March of 2011. It was a rough six months to say the least, and yet I made it through.

If you're wondering how I did it, I'll do my best to explain. It wasn't easy. It took a lot of strength, tears on the neck of my horse, and spirituality to get me through, but I always knew that God had a reason for putting me on that path.

I should preface this story by saying that I am a strong person, emotionally and physically. You wouldn't know it to look at me, since I look like a petite little thing. But I think God did that to force me to prove myself, and that's what I have always done.

I grew up with very blonde hair so endured "dumb blonde" jokes from a very young age. I was small so got teased about how tiny I was, until I grew to be 5'4" and that stopped. I got the "too pretty to be anything worthwhile" comments, too, and soon I was doing everything I could to prove myself. I pushed myself to go to college. I pushed myself to join the Army because I wanted to see if my body could handle it as a 28-year-old woman. I pushed myself to be a good friend to people who could have cared less about me. And I pushed myself to be an amazing daughter to my dying mom.

The thing is, I don't regret pushing myself or showing my strength because it showed me exactly what I am capable of, and that is a whole lot more than anyone ever thought. It also showed me that everyone is capable of more. My mom was my catalyst and role model. She showed me what it is to be a strong and capable woman, that all of your dreams are possible, and that you can overcome any obstacle. I will forever be grateful for her lessons.

Losing my mom was the biggest shift that ever occurred in my life. I had to learn to live without her advice, support and friendship. She was my rock; she was the one who gave me wings to fly and pushed me to be better than I thought I could be. She helped me when I was down, and celebrated me when I was up. She gave me faith in God and taught me to find the silver lining in everything that seemed bleak. She gave me my sarcasm and my wit, and she made damn sure that I could fit into any crowd, from rednecks to royalty. I struggled without her love and friendship, but made it through by trying to make her proud of everything I did. I focused on raising my two boys, riding my horse, taking care of my home, going back to school part time, and being a good wife...or so I thought.

Turns out, my husband didn't agree with the "being a good wife" part, and by February of 2011, he had not only asked for a divorce, but told me he had a girlfriend, too. He said he'd been waiting a while to tell me, had wanted to tell me sooner, but that when he finally was about to, he couldn't because I was still crying over the loss of my mom. He said he waited until he just couldn't wait any longer. Well, that was a huge slap in the face.

The funny thing was that I didn't really care about losing my 10-year marriage; I was only concerned about my boys and how it would affect them, and whether I would be able to keep my horse. My heart broke for my boys but in my soul I felt relief. Our marriage had never been full of trust or love, so it didn't feel like a big loss to me. Instead, I was very afraid. There was fear around how I would pay my rent, pay for my kids' basic needs, and whether anyone would hire someone who'd been a stay-at-home mom for the last 5 years.

Getting a job was terrifying! I had to learn to talk shop again and put together résumés that didn't look nearly empty. The only thing I had any current experience in was kids and animals. So, guess where I got a job: at a veterinary hospital as a receptionist! I got to be with animals and do stuff I already did as a mom, like scheduling appointments, paying bills, and cleaning up. It was perfect!

I had also met a new man who was so sweet and caring. He loved me like I had never known before. The good life didn't last long though. I started getting harassed at work and going there became unbearable. I wasn't sure how I was going to do it but my boyfriend supported my decision to leave my job, and he helped me through it. I was able to stand my ground and I even made a case for unemployment and won.

This was a helpful step in the right direction, proving to myself that I was heading down the right path. That may seem strange, but after so much loss I needed every small win I could get, and I practiced gratitude for those small wins. My self-confidence had taken a hard hit in my previous marriage and I really needed to know that I was heading down the right trail. I needed God to hold my hand, but I wasn't actively asking Him to do that...yet.

My boyfriend, who is now my husband, supported me through those difficult times and helped me to see that I needed to treat myself better, not staying in toxic situations out of fear. He was the first person to help me see that I didn't need to sacrifice my well-being just because I was afraid to move. He helped me learn to trust men again and embrace change. He helped me go back to school to earn my Bachelor's degree and then again to earn my Associates degree in Veterinary Technology.

Even in the past year, since the first edition of this book was published, so much has changed. It's unbelievable when I look back. There are things that I dreamed would never happen that became reality, and others I wish I could just make better with the snap of my fingers. Huge house moves, healing karmic lessons, and changes in parental custody, just to name a few!

See, I like to do things backwards, or
rather, in a circular fashion. The great thing that I
learned about going in circles is that even though
it feels like you're back where you started, you're
really not. You've grown; you've spiraled up and
out and see everything below you with a new
perspective. Just like when you circle your horse;
you're showing them that it's not okay to move
forward unprepared, pedal to the metal. You've
got to take it slow, circle around a few times, get
your bearings, your feet under you, and start off
on the right lead.

See, everything I have done over the last
10 years has been to have a career working with
horses, but not as a horse trainer. I was already
too old for training and had too little experience.
I tried lots of other ways to get to that point but
those ways didn't always fit either. The jobs
were either paying too little, too far away, or
there were too few vacancies and tons of more
qualified applicants. Although those options
didn't work for me, they did lay some serious
groundwork for the beautiful path that I'm on
now.

Along this circuitous path towards my
horse career, there has been one "person" who
has helped me, guided me, and supported me

over the last 10 years. She kept my horse passion burning bright just by being herself, and that is my mare, Paris. She is more than just a mare or a horse to me. She is my best friend, my twin flame, my heart horse. You can call it whatever you like. Me? I call it family.

She and I had a few accidents that really destroyed my confidence but, in all honesty, I had no confidence in any part of my life before she joined my family. My marriage kept me weak, my thoughts held me back, and my fears kept me down. Paris was probably the first connection I had that gave me some confidence and allowed me to trust and feel my way forward.

Our first meeting was like two souls seeing each other again after many years apart. We connected instantly. She's been with us since my oldest son was just 2 and a half years old. He grew up with her and learned how loving horses can be. She protected me from our two young, rambunctious horses when I was pregnant with my second son, and she let me cry on her withers when my mom passed away. She was the one who consoled me during my bitter divorce. She was there when depression set in whenever my boys were away visiting their dad, and she always waited patiently for me to be ready to ride again.

Our first accident together was also our first ride together. It was 2007 and it was an epic case of extreme ignorance, coupled with a seller who just wanted to drop her off and run. I had minimal adult experience with riding, saddling, or handling horses. I had gone on a couple trail rides with a friend but everything had been done for me then, so other than getting on, I hadn't done much. I'd also had a pony when I was 8, but again everything had been done for me.

So, when Paris arrived at the boarding facility I allowed her a few days to acclimate before my ex and I threw the saddle on. But I jumped on too quickly with the saddle left loose and the stirrups super short. I held on with my legs, but as she went faster I got scared not knowing how to stop her. My ex yelled for me to jump off, so I did, falling hard into a wall, dislocating my shoulder and pounding my knee.

Needless to say, I felt really stupid and cried because I hadn't known what to do. Paris was the best little two-year-old horse, standing there in the round pen with the saddle rolled under her belly, waiting for me to help her. I was deeply ashamed. She was not at fault in any way, and I never blamed her, but my ignorance caused me to develop a severe lack of confidence in every part of my life.

Through working on releasing my fears, I learned to let that all go, and to understand that it was all part of my learning curve. It was a part of my journey that I needed to endure in order for it to wake me up...and it worked *big time*. After that accident, a wonderful trainer took me under her wing for a brief time and taught me all the basic foundational work that I needed to know.

I didn't have another accident on Paris until around 2014, nearly 7 years later. We were on a trail ride with a friend and I was practicing opening the gate while mounted. The problem was, I had to lean way down, unlock the padlock and chain, and then open the gate inwards to get through. Everything was going well: lock was done, gate was opening, but I couldn't extend my arm wide enough to let us through. Paris got partway through the gate but when she couldn't go any farther she pushed through hard. I lost my balance and fell off, and she took off running down the trail towards home. I had twisted my knee during the fall when my foot got stuck in the stirrup, but I wasn't seriously injured. I got up, dusted myself off, and started walking home.

Within 5 minutes, Paris came trotting back, looking at me like, "What happened? Are we going home now?" She really is the best little horse. Though it wasn't a serious accident, again my confidence was rocked. I was afraid to trail ride after that. The problem was, in 2014, I hadn't yet learned crucial healing techniques, and so I was very timid about riding and never felt like a confident and comfortable leader for my horse. I let Paris carry me, literally and figuratively, emotionally and physically. I just wasn't there yet, and so I had to struggle through my fears to get back on Paris.

Now, I was very aware that I was struggling with fear around my horse...but I was also struggling financially. I didn't have money to hire a trainer or a coach to help me, but I *did* have extra time and the ability to use my muscles. I looked for a job where I could clean stalls in exchange for training, either for me or for my horse.

A local, well-known, female trainer was looking for a work exchange, and not only did I learn from being in contact with multiple horses daily, but also from cleaning, turning out the horses, and helping her with the marketing side of her business as well. In return, Paris and I received riding training, and what I learned in that time catalyzed my current success with my horse. My confidence grew, and my relationship with Paris developed. It was a huge step in the right direction.

Then, in 2015, a friend of mine urged me to have a Tarot or Angel card reading with a very specific woman who lives in France. I'd had a few Tarot readings with my mom when I was a teenager, and a few more before I had my kids. I'd always felt a connection to the Tarot and had tried to learn it as a teenager, but I wasn't old enough to understand it then. When my friend suggested I have a reading I thought, "Okay, let's give it a shot. It can't hurt right?"

Well, it turns out that this woman in France is a powerful and gifted healer, and it *did* hurt, a lot. It hurt because I had to face all my fears and learn to forgive. I had to forgive my ex-husband who cheated, lied, and did everything he could to hurt me. I had to forgive all the people in my past for leaving me behind, forgive my mom for dying, and especially–and probably most importantly–I had to forgive myself. I had to forgive myself for not leaving my marriage on my own terms, for missing my mom so much, for not being successful like other women were, for not bringing in any money, for never having the little girl I'd always wished for, for not having any friends, for being an introvert who didn't fit in, and for being ME. That was a lot of work. It didn't happen overnight but in about 6 months' time, my life had drastically changed.

It was now late 2015. I was riding my horse with newfound confidence, reconnecting, and proving to her that I was now capable of leading us both and that she didn't need to be the leader in our relationship anymore. Our relationship had grown and changed over the years, getting stronger and better with time thanks to proper training combined with the self-healing techniques I'd learned.

The year that I turned 40, my husband and I decided to breed Paris so he could have his own custom-built horse, but right at the end of that year, I found out I was pregnant. Yep, I was finally going to have that perfect, healthy little girl that I'd wished for. The change in my life was so dramatic that it was almost unbelievable. I was expanding my family by adding two more members: one equine baby and one human baby.

It was a drastic change to my life path, but I was fully ready to embrace it. I had worked really hard on releasing my fears, moving towards forgiveness, and promoting love in my life in a big way. It just goes to show you that when you have someone to guide you along the way, it can create rippling shifts and changes in your life.

It felt like God was rewarding me for doing His work. I had always been a believer in God, angels and Jesus, but I didn't always know how to do what God was asking of me. I didn't know I could connect energetically until I met those key people along my path who showed me how. The healer showed me how to meditate, how to connect to the angels, ask them questions, and understand their answers. She helped me to believe in myself more than I ever had before.

In that same year, in one of the healer's workshops, I met the next soul who would become my friend, influencer, and coach as well. She and I were continuously being put together for partner work in this workshop, and I think it was because the healer knew–consciously or unconsciously–that we were highly connected and would need each other in the future. More than once, this new friend and I even showed up for the workshop's video calls wearing matching clothes.

My new friend helped me fully embrace my ability to read energy–or "Chakras" as they're called–and she helped me learn Tarot cards, too. This woman also, in part, helped me to become the person I am today. She is the person who showed me that anything is possible, that amazing changes can happen quickly when you embrace them, and that you need to be YOU. She taught me how to be a coach, how to start my business, and then introduced me to book writing.

And this is where I am now: writing this book for you to read, owning my life story, and speaking up to share my message of healing from fear though equine empowerment. After such a journey, I'm ready to be of service, which is why I'm here sharing my message with you, as well.

To this day, I continue to meet new lightworkers, healers, and wonderful people who inspire me to continue my healing journey. Some of them are horse owners or horse lovers and some are not, but they all show up along my path for a reason. I have learned to just trust and you can, too. Trust in God's plan, trust in your intuition, and in yourself. You are enough and you have everything you need inside of yourself to be successful.

You may not realize at first that when a person is put in front of you it's so they can make a difference in your life. If you're open to receiving, you'll find yourself meeting interesting people and connecting the dots as to how those people fit into your story. I would not have been ready to embark on such a journey without all the wonderful people in my life, especially my Paris. Every day she shows me how to be nonjudgmental, accepting, and loving of everyone. She especially taught me how to forgive myself and not dwell on the mistakes of my past.

Now, I don't claim to be the perfect horse owner, rider, or person in general, and I don't aim to be. I think making mistakes and failing means that you're successful! You're successful at trying and pushing forward, making attempts, and taking chances. If you never try, you can never succeed. So, if you're trying, you're already succeeding and that's all that matters. I hope that, whatever the experiences you've had with your horse, you choose to see these experiences as part of your awakening, part of your journey on this life path. Hang in there and get ready to shift!

Even I have shifted so much since the first edition of this book was published. If you read the first edition, are you able to look back and notice significant changes in your life since then, too? Or, if you didn't read that first edition, can you look back over the past year and recognize the changes that took place in your life?

Oftentimes we focus solely on our physical changes, or on our achievements or failures, but there is so much more to recognize as well. Look for your emotional changes, changes in your daily habits, or even changes in the way you think. Reflect on them, really SEE those changes, and love them because without change there is only stagnation. Growth cannot occur.

And just remember that everything is a journey, and no one has a perfect life. No one is what you assume they are, no one deserves to be judged or criticized, especially if you're doing it to yourself. We're all just trying to make it here on earth every single day. Keep your head up, your back straight, and keep changing and growing.

At this point you may be wondering about the origin of my methods. They are a combination of my life lessons, my education, and my own healing experiences.

When it comes to horses, I learned about the importance of body language by studying ballet for more than 20 years. Then, through my degree in Veterinary Technology, I had access to internships that taught me, in-depth, about equine body structure, dynamics, and nutritive requirements. Finally, I became certified in Equine-Facilitated Learning by the HERD Institute in early 2019.

And when it comes to coaching and counseling, my degree in Middle Eastern and Religious Studies gave me a foundation of cultural awareness, and a scholarly approach to spirituality and the soul, which is important in any kind of coaching or healing work. On top of that, I'm in the process of completing my Master's degree in Marriage and Family Therapy.

I have been blessed to find this path and now spend my days doing all I can to help others in every way I know how. I developed the techniques in this book through tried and true methods. My clients have used them and have achieved success. I feel confident that these techniques will help you achieve your goal of reconnecting with your horse, too.

However, if the techniques I'm going to describe in the next chapter feel too difficult for you to tackle on your own, I urge you to find a qualified friend to help you or to contact me directly if you'd rather more personalized help. It is not failure if you can't do these exercises right away. I only see effort and the desire for change.

With that said, turn the page and let's begin empowering you to release your fears with my 10-step solution for CONNECTING to your horse.

Wisdom from Paris

When I ran off after my mom lost her balance and fell, I tried to run back home. But I felt empty and alone and even more afraid. I had to go back and see if she was okay. I couldn't leave her there. My mom has become my family, and we need each other. I let her cry in my mane and she keeps me safe and happy. We may not speak the same language, but we know how to speak the language of love.

Chapter 3: My 10-Step Solution for Releasing Your Fears

"The horse is a mirror to your soul. Sometimes you might not like what you see, and sometimes you will."

~Buck Brannaman

You know those annoying little problems that keep popping up in your life? Those pesky things that throw you off your game and make you feel like a donkey instead of the head mare?

It could be a small thing, like someone making an ill-timed snide remark, or it could be a surprise bill showing up in your mailbox. It could be a client canceling when you were counting on that money coming in, or it could be more serious, like finding out your horse is lame because you forgot to check her feet. And maybe she's just got a rock in her shoe, but you're beating yourself up because you forgot to check and you are normally so diligent with her care.

These sorts of issues are often symptoms of a much deeper problem, and I've developed my program to help you tackle that problem at its core. Let's call that problem out by its name: *fear.*

For the purpose of making it easier for you to remember, I've given the steps to this program the acronym of CONNECTING. Just like a horse needs to be connecting with the horses in her herd, we need to be connecting with every aspect of our lives. We should be connecting in our relationships, connecting with our finances, connecting to our spiritual beliefs, connecting with our horses and other pets, and so on. Without connecting and feeling authentic in all areas of our lives, we feel the disorganization or the disunity; nothing functions optimally.

Is this how you've been feeling, with your fear of riding your horse? By connecting within your life, you *can* find what the horse finds through connecting energetically with her herd: *balance.* And balance within your life is one of the biggest steps toward conquering your fears.

CONNECTING is like an acrostic or word puzzle. Each letter stands for the first word in the title of one chapter of this book. For example, the first "C" represents Chapter 4's title, "Could it be Me?" and so on. Ten may seem like a lot of steps, but that's why I created this simple way to remember them all. It's much easier to remember CONNECTING than to remember all ten different steps! See, I've got your back! Read on for more details on CONNECTING and how the program works.

"C" stands for the first step in the program, which is asking yourself, "Could it be Me?" The fact is that each and every one of us has been through some ordeal in our lives. Maybe you had a hard fall off your horse, or some other traumatic event. Maybe you've had a lot of death in your family, divorce, pregnancy loss, PTSD, abuse, homelessness, or any number of things that you've been carrying with you. Maybe it's something less dramatic but still traumatic to you, like the death of your favorite horse and how that won't allow you to connect with your new horse. Maybe you have a horrible boss, or a ton of anxiety and stress that you just can't let go of. It doesn't matter what the pain is called. The fact is, it's pain.

The way we handle our pain can very easily define who we are. If you feel the pain deeply and become depressed by it on a regular basis then you need to heal the source of your pain in order to move forward into your brilliant and abundant future. Without healing the history of your pain, you will hang onto these wounds and they will undermine your every step. If you're reading this book then you know what I'm talking about. The pain of a heavy heart is sitting there inside your body and it's undermining your self-power. You may be thinking, "That's not me. I don't do that." but I'm guessing that when you need your confidence to be at its best, there always seems to be something niggling at you, making you feel unworthy or unable to be "your best." We all have something, so don't be afraid to embrace it. Embracing it is the first step to healing it.

"O" stands for "Opening to Forgiveness," which is Step 2 of the program. Forgiveness is the key to happiness in this world. To offer someone true forgiveness means that you have to look deep inside yourself, release your pain and find love for the person or thing that hurt you. Forgiveness is a kind of love, but don't be confused. It's not about showing love to the person who hurt you; it's about loving yourself enough to allow love and forgiveness to take the place of the pain in your life.

"N" stands for "Never Letting Fear Win," which is Step 3. Fears are something that every single one of us have, just like we have pain. Some of us are afraid to lose control of our horse, others are afraid to even mount. No matter what your fear is, conquering it is another way to

bring out your inner power and establish a stronger sense of confidence within you. The divine does not want you to be afraid of your power or abilities. He wants you to use your gifts to help others and help yourself. If you allow your fears to take over, you are doing a disservice to both your equine friends and to yourself.

"N" is for Step 4, "Nailing a Positive Mindset." This chapter covers how important your mindset is, not only to your daily life, but to successfully accomplishing anything that is required of you. This chapter also talks about how being open-minded can allow you the freedom to change your destiny. Moving mountains with your mindset is something that can bring you to a new way of thinking and achieving. Imagine the positivity you can bring to your daily visit with your horse if, in your mind, you're already set for a great encounter.

"E" stands for "Embracing Love, Healing Energy, and Magic." In Step 5 we delve into the physical, emotional, and spiritual aspects of your body and life. Everyone is lovingly affected by nature, animals (especially our horses and their energy) and universal positive energy. This

chapter teaches you how to embrace the healing process and how to apply it to your everyday life.

"C" stands for "Counting On Your Intuitive Confidence." Do you love yourself? Can you feel positive about your own attributes? Are you self-aware? Can you self-reflect and see how far you've come in your life, where you went wrong and where you did just right? Step 6 teaches you that there is more to your life than just what's on the surface. Intuitively learning to FEEL your way forward is so important in your healing journey. It's time you trusted your intuition with confidence.

"T" stands for "Trusting the Divine and Finding Your Balance." Step 7 teaches you how to allow space for divinity, love, and success to enter your life. Divine love can come from anywhere and anyplace that speaks to you. You can be a nature lover, animal lover or just someone who loves to help others. You can feel it every time you hug your horse. It's that feeling of unconditional and non-judgmental love, and it's an important part of your healing journey.

"I" asks the question, "Is Your Relationship With Your Horse Strong Enough?"

And in Step 8 you'll learn different methods for bonding with your horse, and how to strengthen your bond if it's not as strong as you'd wish it to be.

"N" stands for "Notes for Those with Disabilities, Competitive Riders, and How to Connect with Other People's Horses" and in Step 9 we discuss how those with disabilities can begin to get reacquainted with horses in a safe and positive manner, how competitive riders can tackle some of their own fears, and how anyone can connect with a horse they do not own.

"G" comes in with the final, tenth step of CONNECTING, and that is "Giving Up is NOT an Option." In this chapter we'll discuss how life is always going to throw obstacles in your path, and there will be times when you want to give up, but giving up *cannot* be an option for you if you want to succeed at connecting with yourself and your horse.

So that's CONNECTING, the 10-step solution that you will be implementing throughout the rest of this book. But before you begin, I want to talk to you about how to make all these steps work for you and how best this program can help you get back in the saddle, or at least reconnected with your horse and yourself.

As I discussed in the last chapter, I strongly suggest that you use journaling as a tool when working through the ten CONNECTING steps. And because I want you to get the *most* out of this program, I've created specific journal prompts that correlate to each of the ten chapters that teach you all about CONNECTING.

Each of these journal prompts has two parts: a reader-related question and a horse-related question. These prompts have been designed to help you put pen to paper, and write through your feelings and experiences. The "reader" prompts are meant to help you find where you're at in your life: how you're feeling, where you may be hiding fear or pain, and much more. The "horse" prompts are meant to help you discover how your horse may be feeling: where your relationship with your horse is strongest or weakest, and more.

Rest assured, however, these specialized prompts are completely optional and you do NOT *have to* use them. They're simply a tool to help you along your adventure of self-discovery. If you'd rather not use my prompts, still want to try journaling, but are unsure if you can come up with your own prompts, what you could write about instead are your own thoughts and feelings: how you felt that day, what your bond was like, maybe even how your ride went!

The idea is just to get you writing and riding so you can begin connecting, inside and out. But know, too, that you don't *have to* journal at all to still benefit from the CONNECTING program. Whatever you choose to do will be what is best for you at this junction in your life.

This book also provides you with various exercises throughout for you to complete. Depending on how much time and energy you have to invest, most of the exercises have both a full version, and a "lightning" version. Meaning, if there's ever a day when you're in a hurry or simply don't have the energy or resources to commit to completing the full version of an exercise, the lightning version gives you an option that requires less time, fewer or no supplies, and can mostly be done in your head.

Not every exercise has a lightning version though, so be prepared. You *will* have to do some of the exercises full out. You should also note that the lightning versions of the exercises may not be as effective as the full versions. What I recommend is that if you feel as though you're not getting the results you want from doing the lightning versions, go back as soon as you are able, and do the full versions instead.

And right here and now I want you to actually commit to doing these exercises. Yes, that means you will need to carve out time in your overloaded schedule to achieve results. What I can tell you though, is that you will be so thankful you made that time for yourself and got to the root of your problems.

I'm guessing you're great about making sure you do all the activities and therapies that your horse requires, but when it comes to taking care of *you*, I bet it goes right out the window. (Unless it prevents you from riding, and even then, you're back in the saddle pre-doctor approval, am I right?) In fact, I bet this lack of self-care has become somewhat of a habit of yours. You call the vet when your horse lays down for too long because he might be trying to colic, but if you trip and twist your ankle in the pasture you won't see your own doctor. Your horse looked at you funny or pinned his ears at you while you braided his tail and now you have the animal communicator coming to talk to him to discover his feelings, but you haven't explored your own feelings or had a good cry in years.

I can tell you right now, if you do not put some time and effort into yourself, you will come falling down, if you haven't already. There is so much that you do each and every day for everyone else. When does the time come for you to show *yourself* a little love? You MUST love yourself for the love to keep flowing from you into others. If you show yourself the amount of love you show to others, you will be surprised at how quickly your life will start to change. Loving yourself starts the chain of dominos falling into place. It IS what ultimately will get you back in the saddle and reconnected with yourself and your horse. So start showing yourself some love by committing to do these exercises–and the healing work that goes along with them–for your sake *and* for the sake of your sweet horse.

When doing the exercises in this book, grab yourself some candles, maybe some flowers, and crystals are awesome, too. Definitely bring some essential oils, and then find a quiet place where you can go and be alone to do your self-care. Allow yourself this time for peace, sanctity, relaxation, and self-love. Find yourself, free yourself from your worries, ease your mind, and let go. There is no rush. The world can wait but you cannot. Remember to be thoughtful and feel your emotions. If you need to cry, it's okay to. You're in your sacred space and you can let your emotions out. Set up your sacred supplies in a way that sings to you and then let it be. It doesn't have to be perfect; it just has to BE, just like you.

Making time for YOU is a necessity, not a luxury. Yes, being with your horse feels like "you" time, but a lot of the time it's not; it's really about your horse. It IS a great time for connecting to your horse, but you need time to be alone, relax, and find yourself so you can be authentically you with your horse.

Have you ever stepped into your horse's personal space and thought, "Who am I?" In a strange way being that close to your horse will bring out those feelings of needing to discover your own depth, your own authentic self, or to drop the façade that you wear everywhere else. You need time alone to reconnect with yourself and rejuvenate. "You" time will help you to remain fully in the present moment with your horse. It will help you to find peace, balance, and the ability to push past any obstacles you may be encountering.

This 10-step program is meant to help you in more than just one way. If you take the time to do the exercises and read the book, you will see a change in yourself, in your horse, in how your horse responds to you, in your personal life, and in your relationships in general.

See, this is not your typical "get back to the basics, because starting your foundation training all over again is going to fix everything" book. I don't do that. What *I* do is break it down for you, because generally the problem is YOU. Yep, that's right. And please don't be offended because I speak the truth. It is you that needs attention, not your riding techniques, your tack, your horse's training, or anything else. You need to focus on what thoughts, feelings, and fears are keeping you from your horse. And it may be hard work but it's worthwhile hard work, isn't it?

Journal Prompts for Each Chapter

Chapter 4:

1. *What is my story? What has brought me to where I am today?*

2. *Where am I with my horse(s) today and how did I get here?*

Chapter 5:

1. *What do I want my life to look like?*

2. *What would I like to accomplish with my horse(s) in the next 6 months?*

Chapter 6:

1. *In week one, you wrote about your story. Looking back, can you pinpoint where your fear originates from?*

2. *Write about one action your horse does that contributes to your fears and prevents you from being bold and confident.*

Chapter 7:

1. *What changes would I have to make in order for my life to look like my dream life?*

2. *What does my ideal relationship with my horse look like?*

Chapter 8:

1. *What is one thing you wish you could be forgiven for?*

2. *If you had made the choice to get back in the saddle earlier, where do you think you'd be with your riding and/or your relationship with your horse?*

Chapter 9:

1. *Write about one person or thing that inspires you to either be a better version of yourself or to take action towards your dreams.*

2. *Reflecting on your relationship with your horse, also considering his herd life, do you think your horse is happy?*

Chapter 10:

1. *Write down 7 affirmations that make you feel strong, confident and happy.*

2. *Write down 5 ways you can show your horse more love, trust and respect this week.*

Chapter 11:

1. *What are five thoughts that you can change into positive ways of thinking in your everyday life? (Ex. "I'm going to be scared to ride today" into "I'm going to be brave and calm my fears when I see my horse today.")*

2. *Write three attributes that you love about your horse.*

Chapter 12:

1. *How do you relax? Write down five ways that you can achieve full relaxation that do NOT include your horse.*

   2. *Write a list of ways that you can relax with your horse that do not include riding.*

Chapter 13:

   1. *Write a letter to yourself to read one year from now. List what you hope to have accomplished and what changes you hope to have made.*

   2. *Write or find a letter, poem or short story and take it to the barn to read to your horse(s). Observe your horse's response.*

Final Prompt:
   1. *How has applying this process moved your relationship forward with your horse?*

Wisdom from Paris

Sometimes my mom brings people to see me and, boy, are they strange! Some are really sad and some are pushy and some are really scared of me. They don't seem to know how to fix themselves, so I just give them a little reminder of what they look like to me. That usually seems to work. But now, all of a sudden, I've got a job and they call me an "equine coach." (Whatever that is!)

Chapter 4: Could It Be Me?

Horsemanship is the art of mastering our own movements, thoughts, emotions, and behavior. Not the horse's.

~ *Mark Rashid*

This is the question that you will continue to reflect on as you do the exercises in this chapter. The purpose of the exercises in this chapter is to really get down to the root of your problem and discover your patterns of behavior, emotion, and thought.

There are quite a few exercises in this chapter, so please give yourself enough time to do the work. You will come away with a much deeper and better understanding of yourself, and hopefully a clearer vision of how you became who you are today.

Why do you need to know that? Because you need to know why you act the way you do. Why do you have fear in your heart where there should be love? Why do you blame yourself, your horse, or your past for what's going on in your present? This is your chance to find out. Let's get started.

Have you ever thought about everything you've been through in your life? Have you actually sat down and reflected on the past? The trials and tribulations, the joys and sorrows, the grief, the losses, the bliss, and the boring have all had a deep impact on your life.

Remember the birth of your first child and the pure love you felt at that moment? Or the day your mom died and the deep inward sadness you felt? Or the wonder of your first time touching a horse, and the pain and frustration you felt falling off for the first time? These and more are the critical moments in your life that have shaped who you are today.

There are so many experiences in your life that really, truly have shaped you over the years. The foundation you learned–or didn't learn–from your parents and teachers, and your childhood friendships and experiences, all have had a tremendous effect on your personality.

Some kids have the most beautiful childhoods, some have mediocre ones, and others have horrible ones. Those experiences really change who you become, and you can't simply forget or ignore them. They show up in your daily life through the decisions you make, and the actions you choose to perform. They will affect whether you choose to take one career path over another, how you relate to one human being more than another, which horse you connect to and why, and just how you live your life in general. Every little thing you do is dictated, in some form, by the adventures or misadventures you had in your earlier life.

It really is incredible just how much your experiences shape your life. Reflect back on some of your own experiences; can you pinpoint some of those life-shaping moments? Here's another example that you may have experienced but may not have thought of at first as life shaping: having to work from a young age to help support your family. That simple job could have propelled you to become a hard worker or even an overachiever. Growing up with less can put some people on the path to desiring success at an extreme level, whereas growing up with money can lead others to lack empathy for people who are less fortunate.

There are so many ways that life's various events can affect your adult life. I'm sure you have many thoughts running through your mind right now as you put together the pieces of why you are where you are in your life right now. Exercise One will help you make sense of all these thoughts.

Exercise One: Weighing the Positives and the Negatives

Full Version:

I want you to grab your journal or a piece of paper and jot down some of those life events that you feel have shaped you into the person you are now. The events that have caused drama in your life, the ones that you may not want to remember, or the ones that were so glorious that you could never forget them. Write them all down in two columns: one column for negative events, and one for positive events.

Next, I want you to look at those columns. Do you see a pattern? Do you have more negative events listed, or positive events? Do you see specific events that you know, without a doubt, have shaped the life you're currently living? Circle the ones that have definitely changed your life. You'll be taking a deeper look at those ones.

Remember, it doesn't matter how many or how few you have, it's the quality that counts.

Do you think you have them all written down? If you think of more, you can always come back to this exercise and add them in later.

Now, if there *was* a pattern, what was it about it that you noticed? Maybe there are some events listed that are still really bothering you? Maybe you've listed some really old experiences that are reopening old wounds, making you feel really bad about yourself? Maybe you're still wondering how that experience could have happened to you? I want you to know it's okay; I'll help you address these painful old wounds in a later exercise. For now though, I want you to just notice which of the events that you circled had a really large impact on your life.

And maybe you've thought of circling all of them, and that's okay, too, because now you're going to categorize them. In the negative column, I want you to rank them in order from most traumatic to least traumatic. Then in the positive column, rank those from most happy to least happy. Do any overlap? Maybe some feel bad that should feel good? It's okay and very normal for some things to feel bad, like the remarriage of one of your parents, the birth of a sibling after your parents divorced, or the passing of a beloved pet who used to drive you crazy.

The key is to recognize that these events are ones that shaped you into being who you are today. You would not be the person who is here seeking the help that this book offers if you hadn't had those experiences to shape you. Maybe you believe you would have been a better person without those experiences, or maybe you think that if you'd had it a little easier or been more successful things would be different? But the reality is, those experiences happened and you cannot change them. What can you do? You can accept them, learn from them, and love them for making you who you are right now.

Lightning Version:

Mentally create your positive and negative lists in your head. Take notice of the patterns that you have followed or created in your life. Finally, take the time to really embrace these experiences for making you into the person you are today.

Exercise Two:
Weekly Joy Thoughts

** *Full Version:*

As human beings, we all tend to hold onto our negative experiences, thoughts, and feelings more than our happy or positive ones. Most of us get grumpy, tired, stressed out, and rundown from our fast-paced lifestyles. None of that leads you to be a particularly happy person, and your unhappiness affects those around you. So taking some time to think about your happy experiences can not only lead to a happier day for you, but also for everyone around you. It also leads to a better lifestyle and healthier body, so give it a try and see how you feel.

As I mentioned above, it is very easy to let go of the positive experiences you've had in life, or pass them off as normal everyday occurrences while, at the same time, tending to hold onto the negative ones much too tightly. Why do you hold onto the negative experiences rather than the positive ones? I believe it's because it is easier to stay in the same patterns of thought, belief, and inaction rather than to seek out the positivity and create change.

It's easier to complain about the negative because you find an eager audience, but when you try to share your positivity you are often met with jealousy, anger, or frustration. It is a sad occurrence but one that I find too often reflected in my own life, and in the lives of my clients.

But positivity can bring so much more to your life than negativity, so try to find more of it in your daily life. It's the positive moments that bring you the joy to continue living life in the best way you can. It's the positive ones you need to remember and hold onto, not the negative ones. The negative ones are the ones that need to go. Let them float to the back of your mind for a minute while you reminisce about those beautiful events in your positive column from Exercise One. How do those events make you feel? Do you feel like a different or better person because of those events? Are they capable of bringing you joy just by thinking of them?

If you answered yes, then your assignment for this exercise is to take each of those positive memories that bring you joy and apply them each to a different day of the week. Then, on that day, I want you to think about that particular event every chance you get, at least 10-20 times. For example, let's say you assign the day you got married to Mondays. Then, all day long on Monday, you'd think about the joy you felt on the day you got married.

Continue this practice through all the days of the week until Sunday. At the end of each day journal your feelings about that day and note any differences from what a usual day would feel like. Maybe on most Mondays in the past you've felt grumpy and tired from working all day, but on this particular "wedding" Monday, you feel light and happy and full of energy and love. Note these kinds of differences so that, at the end of the week, you can see how a few joyful thoughts can really change your day.

And, in order to help you stay on track, I've included little reminders throughout this book for you to practice your weekly joy thoughts every day.

**Lightning Version:

Think of a happy thought and focus on that one thought every single day. Do this when you first wake up, at lunchtime, at dinnertime, and just before you fall asleep. Journal what you notice about your experience of each day.

So many people put up walls to try to protect themselves from all these negative feelings and from being hurt by others. Unmindful people who don't take the time to think about their words or actions can hurt your feelings so easily. We'll be going more in depth into this unconscious behavior in Chapter 5, but for now just know that you can be hurt by family members, lovers, friends, colleagues and pretty much anyone else on the planet.

The idea I'd like you to begin to think about here is that the reactive response someone gives to you is a direct reflection of the relationship they have with *themselves*. When someone jumps down your throat, they are usually reacting to the way they feel about themselves at that point in time. It's almost never about you and almost always about them. They don't feel good about themselves and so they don't react well to you.

If you look at these sorts of situations as reflections of them rather than it being about you, then it allows you to feel empathy for that person, rather than anger and hurt. Don't throw up those walls and shut people out; those people who've hurt you are in need of a kind heart, not a cold one. So when someone treats you poorly, rather then putting up a wall and shutting them out, ask them a question about what's going on in their life. They may surprise you with an apology and if not, you'll gain some understanding for another human being.

Exercise Three:
Pinpointing Your Negative
Patterns
(No Lightning Version)

Have you ever noticed that you tend to make the same mistakes over and over again? Take a look at that list you wrote in Exercise One and any patterns you may have noted. Do you see how some of those negative experiences could've been avoided if you had learned from a previous mistake?

If not, let's do another list! I want you to list out any and all mistakes you think you have made in your entire life. This may take some time, so go ahead and do that and come back to this spot when you're finished.

It's hard to remember and list all of your mistakes, isn't it? Well, kudos to you for making the effort to do such a task. Now I want you to look at this list of mistakes and see if you have repeated any of them? How many times have you repeated them? Can you look back at your experiences and tie any of the mistakes on your list to those experiences?

Maybe it doesn't seem like they connect, but they may have happened at roughly the same time and that means there's a correlation. Do you see it? It's there. The same mistakes being repeated that tie back to those negative experiences in your past. Maybe your dad left when you were a child and now you can't seem to meet a decent guy. Maybe you have negative feelings around food because your mom made you eat everything on your plate, and now you struggle with your weight. I could give you a myriad of examples here, but the point of this exercise is to find the connection between the negative events in your past and the mistakes that you keep making as an adult.

Now, not all of those mistakes and bad habits are going to tie to a negative event. Some are just learned along the way, but the events and mistakes that you *can* tie together, please do, so you can truly learn from them, release them, and move on. It is very important for you to know yourself and understand the underlying causes of your fears and blocks.

Now that you've reviewed your repetitive negative habits and past experiences, let's talk about how these things apply to your horse. If you're reading this book it's because you are afraid to ride your horse due to some form of trauma, or you are looking to reconnect with your horse or maybe just with yourself. No matter the scenario, the problem lies within you.

You have a horse that is trained and knows at least the basics of riding, I'm going to assume. If not, the horse may be the problem as well, but this book is only going to focus on you. As we discussed previously, you hold onto negativity more easily than positivity and your horse can feel that. That is exactly why it is SO important for you to do the full exercises if you can, in order to really understand yourself. Once you know what you're holding within you, you can begin to release it and allow those fears of riding to disappear.

Barn Action

Next time you try to approach your horse, whether to ride or just to bond, do a self-check. How are you feeling inside? What emotions are you holding onto from your day or your week? If they're not positive, healthy feelings, then take a couple of deep breaths and release those emotions so that you don't inadvertently pass them on to your horse.

In the following chapters we'll go over, in depth, how to release those feelings for good, but in the meantime, make sure to do a self-check and release before every interaction with your horse. You want every interaction with your horse to be a positive one from here on out. So if you feel like things are going sideways, stop where you are, hug your horse, send him positive love and energy, and go home. It is more important to bond through positive interactions with your horse than anything else. Even if that means that those positive interactions are all you accomplish for the next few chapters, your horse will love you all the more for it.

My hope is that each and every lesson in this book speaks to you and will be easy to implement. I also hope that you will work through any resistance, and that you find yourself in complete alignment, with all of your blocks and fears having turned into love.

But, if you feel like the work I'm asking you to do is too deep or too hard for you to do it on your own, there are other ways to go about getting to the end result. For instance, you can contact me by scheduling a time for us to talk about what you specifically need to get the results you and your horse deserve: dreamwestfarm@gmail.com

My hope is that by the end of this book, you will be basking in the glow of your connection with your horse, and delighting in your newly deepened connection to God. I hope that this will extend to you super confident feelings of love for yourself and others, too! I hope that you successfully get back in the saddle and ride off into the sunset or down the happy trail with all the equestrians and cowgirls cheering your name as you mount up and ride off. I am so proud of you for choosing to do this work for yourself and your horse. When you do the exercises and complete the tasks, you will notice your confidence and connection grow every day!

If this book changes your life and relationship with your horse in any way at all, please drop me a line and let me know: dreamwestfarm@gmail.com

And don't forget to complete the journaling assignments. You can still make great use of them throughout the rest of the book if you haven't started them yet. They act as a sort of diary and a health record for both you and your horse. You can look back and see what was working, what wasn't, and how you both have been feeling. It's never too late to start.

Wisdom from Paris

*Sometimes I have to work hard
when my mom wants to go for a ride
or practice my skills. I LOVE to do those
things, especially when my mom says I did
so good and gives me lots of love and*

*rewards. I work extra hard to be good so
we both have a happy day.*

Chapter 5: Opening to Forgiveness

"Horses are incredibly forgiving. They fill in places we're not capable of filling ourselves."

~Buck Brannaman

In the previous chapter you discovered a lot of things about your past, and all the positive and negative experiences that you have encountered in your life. You made connections that you did not see before and you may have had some painful realizations. Those realizations might also have led to feelings of anger, sadness, loss of love, or even bitterness. Those feelings may be directed toward yourself, or they may be directed towards the people in your past.

See, the emotions you've been feeling may have led you to realize that some of the negative experiences you've had were placed upon you in a needless fashion by parents, friends, your horse, strangers, your spouse, or any other person you've encountered in your life. And you may be feeling the desire to blame those people for what you went through, and that's okay! The blame very well may lie with someone else, but the fact remains that *you* have to deal with the emotions of the experience yourself.

Exercise Four: Releasing Your Emotions

**Full Version:*

In order to deal with these emotions, I want you to take a piece of paper and write down what you're feeling. Who is at fault for what happened to you? Blame them, blame yourself, scream, cry, yell, or mourn if you need to, but let it all out onto that piece of paper. No one will ever read these words but you, so have no fear while you're emptying your heart onto those pages. Let it all out and let it fly.

Why am I asking you to do this exercise? Because all of those negative emotions you're holding inside you WILL turn against you at some point. They will create an unhealthy body, mind and soul. They will poison you until you release them. Even the things you didn't think you'd remember will come up at some point, so taking care of them now will ensure that they don't spring up at an inopportune time in the future. Let's just deal with all the negativity now.

Take a final look and feel at that paper where you threw caution to the wind and blamed your heart out; is it complete? Is there anything else you want or need to add to it? If so, do it now. Get it all out and don't let it poison you any longer. All done? Good. Now let's move on.

For this second part of the exercise, I want you to take that piece of paper that contains a ton of tears, blame, frustration, sadness, hate and anger and either cut it up into tiny pieces or burn it very carefully. This will allow you to watch those emotions become nothing. They will slowly disappear from your soul as you watch the paper disintegrate, becoming smaller and smaller.

Completing this exercise will free you, allowing you to open yourself up to new possibilities. All of that blame, shame, and anger is nothing now but a small pile of dust. Now there is a beautiful place in your soul that is free to be filled with love, light, positivity, and happiness! Check yourself out: how do you feel?

Feel free to journal your feelings about this experience.

**Lightning Version:

Think about everyone who has ever hurt you. The first few people who pop into your mind are the ones you most need to forgive. If you only have 5 minutes, use those 5 minutes to recall the feelings and memories related to your painful experiences with those people. Then visualize the names of your pain inflictors being swept away by a strong wind and being broken into little pieces while blowing away.

I wanted you to complete this exercise because there can be no room in your heart and soul for darkness and negativity. Releasing all of your past hurts also allows you to move into the space where you are ready to forgive. Remember all those people that you just blamed for your pain? It's time to forgive them. Do you feel like you're there yet? I promise, it can be done. You may be feeling raw and uneasy right now, but that's the perfect time to allow yourself to be filled with the light and power of forgiveness.

Think back to your paper from Exercise Four and all those people you listed on it. Were you on there? Was your horse, a friend, a colleague, a family member? Anyone else? Whoever they were, take the time to sit in silence and understand that they are fallible beings. The mistakes you make every day are happening to them, too. We are all imperfect and we all have an effect on each other so, intentionally or not, those people that you blamed were just being human beings, completely imperfect like you and me.

Can you forgive them for being imperfect and wrong? I think the answer is yes, because you would hope for the same forgiveness for yourself if you wronged someone else. People don't come with instruction manuals. Very often we make mistakes in how we treat each other or how we behave in general, and this leads to a lot of pain, hurt, and anger in the world. But, if you can accept the fact that we ALL hurt each other and it's almost always accidental, then it becomes a lot easier to understand and forgive.

Oh, and don't forget to forgive the Universe if you've ever blamed it for your shitty circumstances. That blown tire on the freeway last week was actually due to a bald tire that you've been ignoring. You may be wondering why things always seem to happen to you, or why they seem to happen all at once. "When it rains it pours" is what life may currently feel like, and that may have left you feeling very bitter toward God and spirituality.

You may feel like He is picking on you and making life extra hard for you while your neighbor, brother, or best friend lives a charmed life. I can assure you that the charmed life is not all you are perceiving it to be. I can also assure you that God is not picking on you. All of us are meant to undergo hardships or "tests of life," if you will.

Every one of us here on earth must undergo change and often that change is painful. You may be asking God for a change in your circumstances, such as more money, a new relationship, or a new job. Those requests require a big shift to occur in your life. Your life as you know it must be rebuilt in a way to accommodate your requests. In some areas your life may need complete deconstruction and in others you may just need some simple rearrangements.

No matter what shifts and changes are necessary to accommodate your requests, they constitute growth...and we all know growth is painful. God is listening; He has a path for you. You just have to persist long enough to learn His lessons. Accept His changes and your growth will occur. It will not be easy, but by putting your trust into His plan and doing your best to be kind, honest, accepting, and forgiving, you will find it an easier journey to travel.

Exercise Five:
Finding Forgiveness
(No Lightning Version)

Part 1: Forgiving Others

This exercise will really help you to allow forgiveness to take hold. It's time to take a deep breath and look inside yourself. You need to be relaxed and in balance to perform this exercise. Are you ready to release and forgive? I am here with you; you are not alone. Let's do this together. It is time to heal. You must allow the pain to dissipate as it is released and you surrender yourself to love. To start, I want you to close your eyes and release all the tension in your body.

1. Breathe deeply. As you exhale say, "*I release this pain and surrender myself to love.*" Repeat and again say, "*I release this pain and surrender myself to love.*" One more time say, "*I release this pain and surrender myself to love.*"

2. Now say aloud, "*I invite God to bring me back to a state of love, the love I was born with and carried within me as a child. Heal me from my pain and allow me to see the beauty within me and all around me.*"

3. The final step is to completely forgive others (or the specific person) who has caused you pain. Please say, "*I completely love and forgive _____. I release my anger, fears and pain, and I return to my all-loving soul.*"

Now, you may be wondering why I've asked you to surrender yourself to love and not to peace, or joy, or some other happy emotion. Well, the simple reason is that all other emotions stem from the feeling of love. It is the originator of all positive emotion and from it comes every other good feeling: joy, happiness, excitement, etc.

Getting back to that deepest, most original feeling is the best thing you can do for yourself. Besides, who doesn't want to feel like a loving human soul all the time? I know I want to, don't you? I'm sure your horse would much rather be connected with a loving owner than one who is full of pain and resentment. What if you were a horse? Who would you want riding on your back and kicking your sides, controlling your every movement? I'm sure you'd prefer a loving soul.

Part 2: Forgiving Yourself

There is another side to forgiveness that I want to talk to you about, and that's forgiveness of *yourself* for your perceived wrongdoings and shortcomings. Our perception of ourselves is very often skewed, so I want you to think about all the things that you feel you need to forgive yourself for and write those down.

How do you feel, looking at those offenses down on the paper? Do you think they describe you accurately? Most people are *much* harder on themselves than on anyone else, and usually, what you think are these really horrible faults in yourself end up being not that horrible and certainly not what others see in you.

I want you to repeat the preceding exercise, but now the focus is on forgiving yourself:

1. Breathe deeply. As you exhale say, *"I release this pain and surrender myself to love."* Repeat and again say, *"I release this pain and surrender myself to love."* One more time say, *"I release this pain and surrender myself to love."*

2. Now say aloud, *"I invite God to bring me back to a state of love, the love I was born with and carried within me as a child. Heal me from my pain and allow me to see the beauty within me and all around me."*

3. The final step is to completely forgive yourself and the actions you took that caused you pain. Please say, *"I completely love and forgive myself. I release my anger, fears and pain, and I return to my all-loving soul."*

Now that you have completely forgiven yourself, how do you feel? Do a self-check: is there any pain or fear still hanging around inside you? You can repeat this exercise as many times as necessary until you feel the anger, fears and pain subsiding.

I want you to really understand that your perception of your life and actions is different than what others perceive. I'm sure you can relate to that. You must have some perceptions of people that you came to realize were not even remotely true or correct. For example, your best friend from high school whose life looks perfect on Instagram, but then you meet up for coffee and she tells you that her life is in shambles and she doesn't know how much longer she can keep up the charade.

It's how we perceive each other that can create these feelings of injustice and deprivation that force us to constantly question why our lives aren't better or why our dreams aren't coming true. The reality is, your dreams can only come true and your life can only be perfect if you accept your own reality and create the life you want to live. That's achievable first through forgiveness, then through understanding perception, and finally through understanding what makes you happy and working to make it your reality.

It took me a long time to make this same realization about perception, and I still struggle with it from time to time. Only now I proactively work towards making my dreams my reality, and authentic to me. There is no reason for me to desire or expect what others have, or what they achieve. I only need to do what makes me happy deep in my soul.

Others will always have a perception of me and it's in my best interest to embrace their perceptions as THEIR reality, even when it is not congruent with my own. I must either correct their misperceptions or simply move on and not take it personally. I have always had a hard time moving on when others haven't liked me or when there was an uncomfortable energy in the air. I struggled a lot while growing up when I felt disliked, or if I felt like I wasn't being included in activities.

For example, when I was in high school, I was a cheerleader and hung around the popular group, yet I still felt alone. I only ever had one good friend at a time. I wasn't a "clique" type of person, nor did I have a large group of friends. In fact, the other kids in the school were very intimidating to me. I never felt popular or like I really fit in with any crowd. But then, when I went on our senior class retreat, someone mentioned that they wanted to be like me because I was so popular and nice.

I couldn't believe it! Me, popular? At first, I didn't think the person was talking about me; I thought it was a joke. This was the exact moment that I realized that how you perceive yourself is not anywhere near how others perceive you. And so, in order to get past all this, I had to do a really deep dive into my soul to discover my own truths and knowledge. It wasn't easy and I've had to really mature to get where I am now.

The lesson here: never judge a book by its cover. For example, several of my clients have had severe circumstances leave them with little to no confidence. Even the simple act of saying hi to someone on the street could leave one particular client paralyzed with fear. Other people may have perceived her fear as unfriendliness, which was not the result we were looking for, and so we had to work through that fear.

I gave her the task of saying hi to someone that she didn't know as an exercise to complete, and it was absolutely the most difficult thing I could have asked her to do. When I walked her through attempting this exercise, we talked about ways to make it easier on her, like bringing along a dog to take the focus off of her, allowing her to speak more confidently to strangers. In the past, attempting to converse about herself had often caused her to clam up, frozen with fear, and the perception of this hesitant, guarded behavior was that people thought this poor, damaged woman was being snooty or unfriendly...which couldn't be further from the truth!

It was when we decided to have her engage in conversations about her dog that her demeanor changed and her fear dissipated. She was able to be closer to her true self. This just goes to show, again, how our perceptions of others–or vice versa, others' perceptions of us–can be *very* far from the reality of the situation.

Perception is an individual thing, just like "beauty is in the eye of the beholder." You might see yourself or another person in a particular way, when really the opposite is true. It is always best not to assume or be judgmental. You may think someone is unfriendly or too cool to be friends with you, but in reality that person may be very shy and afraid to speak to anyone.

This is often the case with horses, too. You may look at a horse and rider and think that they have it all together, or you may encounter a pair that seems like the worst combination you've ever seen. Underneath what you see lies a myriad of scenarios. That perfect power couple may be using the harshest, most restrictive bit you've ever seen, and that "worst rider and horse" combo may be just recovering from a fall or injury, or could be newly paired together. Perception is not always reality; remember that. No one, including you, wants to be judged for what you look like. In fact, you probably don't want to be judged at all.

Barn Action

This week, I'd like you to try to take things a step further with your horse. If you've only been grooming and bonding, I want you to saddle her up and take her for a walk. If you're past walking, try to put a foot in the stirrup and stand up on that side. Don't fully mount, just get comfortable saddling, walking and standing up in that stirrup. Do lots of praise, love, hugs, and bonding while you practice standing in the stirrup. Take the focus off of you and your fears, and put it into beautiful attention for your horse.

Remember: instead of focusing on the faults of others–or on your own shortcomings–try focusing on the things you *can* control. Get to know that person who may be struggling, because you're struggling, too, aren't you? Forgive yourself for mistakes, and try to do better. Life doesn't have a "do over," but you can still redeem yourself at any time. So, focus on being your best self and move toward being a deeply loving soul. And remember to give and take credit where it is due, and forgive, forgive, forgive. Forgiveness is the key to life. It creates love where there was anger, and resolves pain even when it seems impossible.

*Reminder: Practice your weekly joy thoughts every day!

Wisdom from Paris

I have bad days sometimes. On those days, all I want to do is stay home, have warm treats, and snuggle with my neighbor. Even on my grumpiest day, I still find a way to be grateful, though. Gratitude reminds me of how far I've come and the beauty my life holds within it.

Chapter 6: Never Letting Fear Win

"Sometimes the mind is like a wild horse. It doesn't know how to behave. If emotions and passions are not controlled, how can you have stillness?"

~Master Choa Kok Sui

Fears are really annoying. They can make you feel like less of a person even though everyone suffers from some sort of fear. You might fear falling off your horse, or getting trampled, kicked, or bit. You might fear failing to win the race, the event, the competition, or gymkhana. You might fear showing poorly, or watching your competitors outperform you time and time again.

No one wants to lose, to fail, or to be seen as someone who doesn't even warrant a second glance. An unskilled competitor who is not a threat to the reigning champ. Logically, you know that fear affects everyone for different reasons, but you may still be ashamed or embarrassed to admit that you're afraid. If you see it as a sign of weakness, try looking at it this way: In reality, fear is just a biological function of your human brain. So instead of being ashamed of it, it's time to start thinking of fear as something that you can absolutely gain control over.

Everyone worries, everyone has fears, and everyone breathes, eats, and uses the restroom. We are all the same, but we can be so different. Fears can really get in the way for some people. Others barely know they have a fear. It's when you aren't doing well controlling your fears that you start to notice a problem. For some people, it's when they start falling behind their friends or other competitors that they discover their fear. They begin to worry that the fear will never go away or that it's their fault.

And guess what: it is. It IS your fault that you allow your fears to get the best of you. It IS your fault that you don't recognize your emotions or choose to change them. And it IS your fault that you lack self-confidence because you allow nonsense to get you down. So, the key here is to change that. Yep, easy peasy; just change it. Stop thinking small. Stop feeling bad for yourself. Stop being negative. Instead, start making a change. The great thing about being willing to change is that every fear can be conquered with the right mindset and diligent practice. You just have to want to do the work and be willing to put forth the effort. Are you that person? Do you want to lose your fears and embrace your beautiful inner confidence? Great, let's get started!

But HOW, you ask? Step One is to start thinking positively. That's when you're going to realize all of the wondrous talents you have and all the things you do that are meaningful and good and right. See, when you start thinking positively about yourself, you begin to believe it. And when you believe it, it becomes your reality. So, if you want a reality that is in harmony with your dreams, you need to start believing and *acting* like the person of your dreams.

If you want to connect with your horse on an unbelievable level, go out and take the initiative to bond with him. Spend that extra time getting to know him. Pamper him and make him love you. The more your horse loves you the harder he will work for you, compete for you, AND the more he will connect to you! Take the time to learn from your horse how to just BE. You can manifest, meditate and channel energy, or whatever you feel it takes to connect to your authentic self and your best friend. So, start to believe in yourself. Be the confident and loving owner your horse wants, and take that step toward your dream relationship with your horse. That's living with ease.

Who are you right now? Do you know? Maybe you define yourself as a mom or a dad, as an equestrian or a friend. Maybe it's your career that defines you or your family life, or possibly it's how many friends you have or how much money you make. No matter how you define yourself, the idea is to make sure you define yourself as good. Not just good at one thing, but good at everything. "Everything" has a broad definition but what I mean is to never doubt yourself: not your worth, not your intelligence and not your strength. We are all good at something, but some of us take a little while longer to feel it.

That person at the barn who is competing every weekend and winning blue ribbons or buckles probably didn't start out the same way you did. And even if they DID start out the same way, they are not the same person as you. They have a different biological makeup with different hormones, genetics, and blood markers. They are unique individuals, just like you are. You simply cannot compare yourself to anyone else on this planet.

You were made imperfect by God as a vessel to carry your perfect soul around and complete your soul's purpose. How does that make you feel? Yes, imperfection and perfection all in one. What does that have to do with defining yourself? It's in knowing who you are that you find the true definition of yourself. I know a few things about you already: you love horses and you're brave. No scaredy-cat tries to ride a thousand-pound wild beast, falls off, and goes looking for help to get back on that beast. Horse people, by nature, are brave and that is something you are darn good at.

You may be asking, "How can you say that? I don't feel like I'm good at anything!" Well you ARE. Not just because you're brave, but because you put forth the effort and learned something. Fears only live in the mind; they develop because of a lack of knowledge. In other words, what you don't know scares you.

The unknown scares all of us. And that's why change is so scary, too, because it brings the unknown into our lives. But you have already begun shifting your mindset, letting go of the fears, and going for it! I'd say that's pretty darn good! You cannot succeed if you don't try and often trying includes failing. You can fail a thousand times, but once you *do* succeed, no one will remember those thousand failures; they will only see the journey to your success. So focus on the journey and not on the failures.

Our society focuses so heavily on whether someone is adept at something rather than on whether they have put forth the effort to learn something new. Learning new things is more important than being adept at something. Why, you ask? First, because those who never try never succeed, but also because learning something new creates new neural pathways and muscle memory. Once you've learned something, it's hard to forget and you've gained another skill to carry with you along your way. It's part of the adventure of life.

If you never fail at something, how can you ever be good at it? If you try and fail, you've discovered something: a way NOT to do that again. You try again and again, and eventually you succeed! That's the beauty of achievement; you find your strengths along the way. Ride the trail, live the adventure. No one will see your falls or your fears, they'll only see the ribbons and buckles.

Belief in yourself: that's Step Two on the path to leaving fear behind. You are only as good as you believe you are. If you constantly say "I can't," then you never will. But if you say "I can," then you will achieve whatever you desire to achieve. It may take a few tries, but if you commit you will get there. Focus on saying "I can" from here on out, and on trying every opportunity that comes your way without letting fear get the best of you.

When I tell you to mount your horse, I don't want you thinking, "I can't do that," or "I guess I'll try to." I want you to say, "Yes, I'm going to do this and it's going to be great." It may sound too easy, but have you noticed that it's really easy to hear all the negative stuff that you're telling yourself, and you just believe it. Why do you think that is? It's because you say it to yourself over and over again. The more something is heard, the more believable it is.

Imagine searching the Internet for "Are horses mean?" If everything you found said that, yes, horses were mean, biting, predatory animals, you'd believe it! You'd probably believe it even if you'd met a sweet horse before searching the Internet. You probably think I'm crazy right now, but seriously, think about how easy it is to read something on the Internet and believe it is real! It's because you are hearing the same information over and over. If you keep telling yourself that it's real and the truth, then it becomes the truth. So, no more "I can't do it," or "I'm going to fall," or "I'm too fat, old, and out of shape," or whatever negative junk you're selling yourself. The truth is, you CAN do it, but only if you WANT to. Make that decision and take action.

As an equestrian, I'm sure that you encounter many fears every day that may get in your way or make you feel emotional. There may be fears of falling off your horse again, of not being able to mount or, even worse, of just not being able to catch or connect with your horse at all. You may be focused on that big event or show that you really need to win at, or else lose your credibility. You may have a lack of self-confidence that's undermining your ability to relate to your horse, or even to get moving in the mornings.

Sometimes life's challenges end up taking over and you don't recognize the effect it's having on you. That is no longer acceptable; you must know what's going on inside of you–how you feel and why–so that you can learn how to work with your emotions. No longer will you be hiding them, or covering them up. Instead, you'll recognize them, own them, and transmute them for the better.

Exercise Six:
Understanding Your Emotions

Full Version:

This exercise is designed to get you to recognize and understand your emotions. I want you to think back to the reason why you became fearful of riding, or why you became disconnected from your horse. If you can't remember, choose another moment in your history where you felt fear. I want you to relive that moment and allow all those emotions to resurface.

Now take your journal and write down the memory, as well as all of the feelings you're currently having throughout your body as you recall the event. How does it feel inside your chest? Inside your stomach? Your head? How does it feel in your legs and arms? Do you feel shaky, lightheaded, out of breath? Is there pressure in your chest, nausea in your stomach, or weakness in your limbs?

Now I'd like you to do the same thing as before, but with a happy memory. Relive the best ride of your life. Feel the air on your skin, your horse's mane and hair on your fingers. Smell the fragrance in the air, or feel the chill in the wind. Pay attention to your body, and as before, write down in your journal all the sensations and feelings you have.

Knowing these feelings will help you to recognize what emotions you're feeling at any given moment, and how your body reacts to them. Once recognized, you will be able to easily transmute them into something more conducive to your present situation. So, work on recognizing and embracing your emotions; they are what make you the beautiful human being you are.

**Lightning Version:

Go to the barn and visit your horse. While you are grooming him, pay attention to the feelings in your body and make a note of them in your journal. Are you feeling completely at ease and unafraid? Are you nervous and jumpy? Do you have butterflies in your stomach, a headache, weak legs? Whatever you're feeling, write it down and continue to take notes about your feelings every time you visit your horse. Recognize any patterns or changes. This will help you discover how your fears present themselves in your body.

Fears are everywhere and they start growing in your mind when you are very young. For example, when I was a kid, I desperately wanted a horse. I had no idea what it took to ride one, care for it, or the cost it took to buy and maintain one, but my parents found a way to get a medium-sized (maybe 11-12 hh) pony from someone local. I was so excited to ride him that I could barely contain myself!

I had absolutely no fear because I had never had a negative experience with a horse before. The first few rides were great because my mom just walked me around, but then I started trying to ride alone and it was really scary. That pony didn't look so big, but the ground felt SO far away when I was up in the saddle! Then, on our walking adventures around my neighborhood, I started getting bucked off all the time. My pony was afraid of dogs, so every time a dog came around, I went flying off into the hard dirt. The first time, I got back on and fear wasn't too present in my young mind. But after the third and fourth fall, I really started to fear riding. Riding represented falling, cuts, bruises, and pain to me.

I didn't have enough positive experiences to outweigh the painful ones. I didn't give up though; I kept riding. Eventually I was doing mini trail rides with my mom's friend. The pony–his name was Sparky–never seemed to connect with anyone though. He wasn't mean but he wasn't loving, and he and I never created a strong bond. Eventually my fears got the best of me, and I told my mom I would never ride again. I had held on for somewhere around 8 rears and bucks, but that last one was the final straw. I still loved horses, but my dreams had been shattered. I wouldn't become interested in riding again for over 20 years.

I have often looked back and cursed that pony, believing that my equestrian history might have been dramatically different "if only." But now, by transmuting those thoughts and focusing on my journey, I realize that everything has happened in the perfect way to bring me right to this point today. I had to endure and transmute my childhood fears in order to be here helping you.

Barn Action

This week, I'd like you to stand in the opposite stirrup if you haven't already. If you have and you are balanced in your stand, try to throw your leg over and just sit in the saddle. You don't have to move; you just need to sit. You can have someone hold your horse if you feel more comfortable with that. Remember that we only want positive experiences with your horse. Little triumphs, not frustrations.

*Reminder: Practice your weekly joy thoughts every day!

Wisdom from Paris

I remember the first day I met my human mom. I had been getting beat up really bad by the other horses where I was living. I had bites all over me, and I was sad. I was only a year old, but I knew the minute I saw her that this human was gentle and kind, and I wanted her to be my new mom. I followed her everywhere to make sure she didn't forget me. I even went to her in her dreams. After a few weeks I was put into the trailer and my dream came true. When I stepped off the trailer, my new mom was there and she whispered in my ear "I couldn't stop thinking about you, Paris." I whispered back, "I know, because I never left your side."

Chapter 7: Nailing a Positive Mindset

"A horse does not greet the sun and say, 'today will be better!' It can only reflect on days of past experiences. It is our job to create a positive past."

~ Karen West

So now that you have released your fears, found forgiveness in your heart, and healed your past experiences, it is time to address the matters of your mind. The mind is such a strong part of your body and has so much influence over your life that it would be inappropriate not to address it.

What you think about and *how* you think about it is more important than you could ever imagine. I'm sure you've met that one person who seemed sad or angry all the time and you really couldn't stand to be around him. That's the type of mindset you want to avoid. What you think about is reflected in your outward energy and personality.

Now, I'm also sure you've met that annoyingly positive person who never does anything but smile and say the most cheerful things. I'm not saying you need to be cheerful all the time–that's not natural either–but ensuring balance is the key. You want to be able to find the positivity in your struggles, embrace the lessons learned in failure or loss, and be ready to jump the hurdles as they come your way with dignity and balance. Balance is what is necessary in all areas of life. Think food, exercise, alcohol, sex and yes, personality and mindset as well.

How do you go about balancing your thoughts? The secret is to think of the opposite emotion to the one you are having in that moment. When you are sad, think of happy memories that support you in your current situation. For example, if you feel angry with your spouse and are thinking of divorce, take your mind back to your wedding. Remember why you married him or her, and bring that memory back to the forefront of your thoughts. It may not fix your problems, but it will bring balance to your thoughts and allow you to be clear and level-headed while you determine how to move forward.

But how *do* you move forward? It is all related to mindset. Again, here is where your understanding of certain words can bring your motivation to a flurry or to a standstill. If you decide that you want your horse's stall to be full of heavy mud, that mud will feel extra heavy, but if you focus on what created the mud–the rain–you will find it easier to complete the task. The rain is a life-giving force, and while it creates mud, it also creates beautiful flowers, green grass, gives us water to drink, and provides your horse with water for a bath or a drink as well. Focus on the beauty of the fact that you get to be with your horse and that the rain is giving life, and that stall will be clean before you know it.

If you are focusing on that upcoming competition and the amount of training you have to put into it in order to win or place, then you're focusing on what feels like a lot of hard work, and maybe even attaching anxiety to your goal. If you continue to focus on the "hard" work in this way, instead of on the beauty in the situation, you will end up with nothing but a participation trophy and a lot of frustration.

But if you instead place the importance on all the quality time you get to spend with your horse doing something you love, and the stronger bond you'll have in the end, you'll find a deeper happiness and ease attached to the training, and you'll find yourself winning that buckle or ribbon. What's even better is that you won't *care* what the actual outcome of the event is because you'll be happy and grateful just to have had the opportunity to show with your best friend. Do you see how powerful your mindset, thoughts, and bodacious brain are? The right mindset can bring you everything you want or nothing you need.

Here's the problem I see that comes up for most people when it comes to mindset: you know you need to adjust your mindset, but you don't know how. You hear talk of changing your mindset. It's a "must do" in all the magazines, on social media, and in the yoga studios, but most of the time they don't teach you how to actually do it. Talk is cheap and practice makes perfect, so how *do* you do it? It's not easy but it's not hard either. It takes work and diligence, and if you are truly willing and you want to change your life, you *will* do the work. If you're not doing the work, you know the answer: You're simply not ready to take control and change your circumstances. That's okay, one day you will be. But if you *are* ready now, let's start changing your mind.

Exercise Seven:
Mastering Your Mindset
(No Lightning Version)

Part 1: Meditation

The first step to changing your mindset is to meditate. Meditation is a real game changer because it quiets the chatter in your mind. When the chatter is silenced you can find clarity within your thoughts, mind. and body. This is why you need to meditate. Does that mean that meditation needs to be a long, arduous task? No, it doesn't. It can be easy and fun and, most of all, relaxing.

There are many types of meditation, and if you seek out and try a few, you'll find one or two types that absolutely work for you. Guided visualization is one type of meditation that you may want to try out. These meditations lead you through some form of visualization, whether it's taking a walk in the park, or sitting on the beach. Alternately, you can use sounds while you meditate, like the all-too-famous "OMMMMM," or there is also tapping which can be very effective. And if you want to incorporate meditation into your exercise practice–or if you need to start exercising in general–you can try yoga. It generally incorporates some type of meditation into each class, as well. Do your own research here, because not everyone likes the same forms of meditation or exercise, so try a few out and choose one or two that work best for you.

Part 2: Gratitude

The next step is gratitude. Yes, that's right. Without gratitude and an understanding of all that you have (or could have), you won't be able to move forward in your mindset to a state where you believe you can have more, be more, or do more. Having a gratitude practice is a simple but effective way to remember just how many beautiful things you have to be grateful for in your life.

What I want you to do for Step 2 is to practice gratitude first thing in the morning every single day, when your mind is fresh and uncluttered. Do this by writing down three things that you are grateful for.

Be creative, think deeply, and don't rush it. This isn't an "I love my shoes, dog, and grandma" type of thing. This is more like, "I am so grateful that I had enough paycheck left over to buy the shoes I've wanted for the last 6 months. I am grateful that my dog keeps me safe and loved when I'm feeling lonely. And I am so grateful that my grandma is so close to me and that we have the beautiful relationship we have."

Do you see how getting specific allows you to feel even more grateful than just rushing through it with minimal effort? Do the work. It makes a difference.

Part 3: Affirmations

Step 3 is to create some daily affirmations. These should include at least one deeply meaningful affirmation every day that makes you feel amazing and worthy. If you feel amazing, worthy, and at your best, your day will be beautiful and happy. Each day pick an affirmation that makes you feel on top of the world. Maybe, *"You are so courageous for taking the leap to change the way you think and feel every day."* Or, *"you have the most kind and gentle heart. Everything you do for others is a beautiful testimony to that."* It could even be as simple as something you just need to hear that day like, *"This new outfit makes you look professional and put together."*

Your affirmations can be anything that really makes you feel special and powerful. You need that power to bring you through each day so that you're motivated to do it all over again the next day. You're also going to be using and creating affirmations as part of Exercise Eleven, so you can choose to use the same ones for both exercises, or make new ones for Exercise Eleven, if you'd prefer. Either way, always choose or create an affirmation that makes you feel strong, worthy and intuitive in the moment you are using it.

These three steps–meditation, gratitude, and affirmations–together with positive thinking, will change your mindset to be exactly where it should be. And what a perfect place to say this:

*Reminder: Practice your weekly joy thoughts every day!

Now that you have mastered the steps to changing your mindset, let's get you manifesting your desires. How do you manifest? By removing the mental and emotional blocks between you and what it is you want, and then by believing, fully and truly, that those things are coming to you. There is nothing that can stop you from getting what you want, except you and your mind. Limiting thoughts equal limiting beliefs, and they limit your achievements, as well.

This is one area where getting back in the saddle can really be hindered. If you question where the confidence, strength, or energy you need will come from, or how on earth you'll actually get those qualities, then they won't come. You have to have faith and trust in God and the Universe that these things *will* be brought to you. If it is in God's plan for you, you will always receive what is yours by Divine right. All you have to do is ask for it, believe it, and expect it. Ask for the strength to reconnect with your horse, believe that you have the right energy to put your foot in the stirrup, and expect that God is going to support you and that you will have an amazing ride.

Expecting it may sound strange or even wrong, but I assure you, it is not wrong. God wants the best for you and he wants to give you all you desire, but you *do* have to put forth some sort of effort in order to receive it or achieve it. I'm sure this makes sense to you; God isn't going to just throw your desires at you because you want them. But, if you display effort and achievements that show you are going to do His will with your requested desire, he's going to get it to you.

Expecting it to come to you is different than hoping or asking. It denotes a belief in God and in yourself, a belief that God sees your worthiness and so do you. If you're just hoping for a better connection with your horse but finding it impossible to believe that you can do it, well, keep on hoping until you finally see your own value and abilities. Then, once you do, BOOM: the money, new saddle, personal qualities you desire, or perfect riding partner will be waiting for you. Knowing your own value is one of the most important keys to success in all areas of life.

These are the keys to manifesting your desires: ask for it, believe it, expect it, and allow it. Make sure you don't have any blocks associated with your desires or your sense of self-worth. If you do, use the Wounded Inner Child exercise and the Releasing Bubble meditation (both to follow in Chapter 8) to let go of those blocks. And be sure to keep your desires at the forefront of your mind; create a vision board, journal your desires every day, write them many times, whatever it is that keeps you thinking about them with ease.

But a word of caution: this is not the time when you want to feel stress, so don't stress out here. Stress will be counterproductive to the manifestation process, producing undesirable side effects, and slowing down or even cancelling out your results. If you're stressed while manifesting money, you'll receive debt and loss instead of wealth and gain. So, don't turn the manifestation process into a negative situation. It's meant to be a loving, trusting, abundant experience that brings blessings into your life. Stay the path and watch the beauty unfold around you.

Allowing what you manifest to flow to you is the crucial final component to manifesting. If you are resistant and fearful of the changes that may come once you receive your desires then you won't be holding space and allowing them to enter your life. It's like entering a dark room and you can't find the light switch. Are you going to wish with all your might that the light switch suddenly appears before you, or are you going to open the door and let light flood the room? Allowing the light to flood the room meant taking an actionable step on your part, but it also gave you exactly what you needed.

Allowing means that you may achieve your desires through inspired thought, assistance sent to you, or unexpected occurrences in your favor. Have you ever thought that you'd like a new set of reins and suddenly a few days later, your friend gives you a pair of reins that she doesn't like or use anymore but they're exactly what you wanted? That is an example of allowing. You allowed that desire to come to you without fear or concern and so the reins appeared effortlessly. You may have to take actionable steps at some points and at others, simply allowing them to flow to you may be enough. I like to think that God is waiting for you to show Him that some of your desires are really what you want and need. Our lives can change so drastically from one day to the next that you may be asking for a new horse to come into your life when the following day you may find out that you're moving to your dream home in Europe and you couldn't possibly transport a horse overseas. The Universe knew what you wanted but couldn't give you both.

Sometimes asking, expecting, and allowing are all that are necessary to achieve your desires, and other times you must take an actionable step like opening the door to flood the room with light. Remember too, that not everything you ask for can be given to you if it's not meant for that point in your life. Allow life to flow, take actionable steps, dream big, ask, expect, and allow. If it's meant for you, it will come to you.

You've released your fears, found forgiveness in your heart, healed your past experiences, and now you've added a positive mindset and the ability to manifest your desires to your toolbox, as well. I'd like to think that, at this point, you feel capable of moving mountains! Doesn't it feel so good to have all those obstacles out of your way? Doesn't it feel amazing to welcome joy and abundance into your heart? Doesn't a healthy and positive mindset feel glorious...or at least a whole heck of a lot better? I certainly hope so! I wrote this book to change people's lives. If your life is changing right now embrace it, relish it, and make note of it. Your awakening journey is officially in full swing.

*Reminder: Practice your weekly joy thoughts every day!

Wisdom from Paris

I find predators everywhere. Everything feels like one to me, but I use my herd energy and the horse senses I was born with to "feel" if something is truly a predator or not. Humans can throw off my senses though, because they look like they are happy but really their energy says they are not. They confuse me because their energy goes up and down all the time. I don't mind if they are sad or angry, everyone has bad days. I just want their inside to match their outside. I've learned that being an equine coach means I can help them learn how to make that match.

Chapter 8: Embracing Love, Healing Energy, and Magic

"Horses carry the wisdom of healing in their hearts, and offer it to any humans who possess the humility to listen."

~Author Unknown

Reading the title of this chapter, you may be wondering, "What in the world does energy and healing have to do with riding horses or competing?" It has a lot to do with it. Many people worldwide are joining in the spiritual awakening that you see happening all around you. You may be looking at your friends, family, and colleagues and wondering if they have started their awakening journey yet. You may be wondering if *you* have. I can assure you, if you are reading this book, you have started on your journey.

If you choose to use your intuition with your horse, which I highly recommend, you will also find that your horse is very helpful in facilitating your awakening and in propelling you forward toward your authentic self and your spirituality. Horses have an undamaged and open connection to God and the Universe. They are wide-open beacons of light and transparency, allowing you to find your path that much faster. This connection and ability that horses have is a beautiful and wondrous thing.

Your journey can begin at any stage of life; everyone is different. For many, it will not even happen in this lifetime...perhaps in another. But you know it's happening for you because you sense that you're different from others. You may be feeling differently, thinking differently, or just having strange occurrences happen that force you to look at life in a new perspective. Maybe you've been seeing number sequences over and over everywhere you look. For example, you look at the clock and it's 11:11 or 1:11, then 2:22, 3:33, 4:44 or 5:55. You may have a receipt and your total is $44.44 or $111.33. These are very common occurrences, happening to people all over the world. Some people think that it's just our brains, programmed to look at the clock at a certain time. Others believe that these occurrences are messages from the Divine, from angels or from spirit guides. I happen to believe that number sequences are messages from the Universe, reminding us that our souls have a job to do here on earth. The message is that we must remember what that job is and take action toward completing our purpose here on earth.

Again, what does any of this have to do with horses? Well, it has to do with the WAY you handle your horses, the way you ride your horses, and the way you train and connect with your horses. This awakening is about becoming more aware of the suffering in the world, of the poor treatment that some of your equine friends receive on kill lots, through "soring" practices, or by being corralled by the BLM.

It also has to do with the people and families that you connect with every day and how you touch their lives. It has to do with focusing on each individual person or horse, and not judging them. Judgment is what propels you into a downward spiral. It brings you to a place of discontent, making you forget that others are imperfect human beings, too. It is the voice of your ego that causes you to look at your friends, family, and strangers in a negative light when you should be holding them in positivity.

We are all supposed to protect, encourage, and love one another, not put each other down. Your horse can easily feel the negative energy that you hold within yourself, or that you direct towards others. That energy will carry over into your interactions with your horse.

But once you are awakened, you also become more sensitive to what's going on around you. You may become more giving, more loving, more focused on others and less self-absorbed. It is about gratitude, giving back, and always being filled with love. You do not have to be a martyr, nor do you have to be poor, homeless, or hungry. But by helping those that are, you will receive more abundance in return: abundance of love, health, friendships, prosperity and goodness.

But why? Why would being a better, more loving person bring more abundance to you? Why would it make any difference unless everything was imbued with energy? It's a scientific fact that the world is completely made up of atoms, which are little particles of energy. If you can understand this, then you can begin to understand how each of your actions and reactions can–and do–cause energetic ripples. So, when you put loving, supportive and positive energy out into the Universe, the Universe sends the same loving, supportive, and positive energy back to you. But if you send out negative energy, it's negative energy that you will get back. It will appear in the form of negative thoughts, damaging events, and loss.

Positive energy brings about positive events, abundance, and happiness. It has been proven that the energy you imbue into your environment is directly related to your emotional state. Energy is emotion and therefore what emotions you hold onto or feel are exactly those ones that you will emit into and receive from the Universe. This science also applies to the manifestation process that we discussed at the end of the last chapter.

Horses are very energetically sensitive beings. They are very in tune with the Universe, with themselves, and with their herd. When you become a member of their herd, they tune into *your* energy, as well. They have to be ready to react and run in order to survive; that means that they must be more sensitive than their predators. Who are their predators? Their predators are big cats, wild dogs, bears, and other carnivores.

If they must be more sensitive than their predators then they must, by necessity, be more sensitive to energy and emotions than humans are. They understand and feel YOU better than you understand and feel yourself. This means that if you want to work together with your horse, then you must be in touch with your energy. This is why the exercises you have done so far in this book have all been about facilitating a better understanding of your own energy; it's been to prepare you to work with your horse.

Why do you think meditation and yoga have been around for thousands of years? And why are they so hot and trendy right now? It is because they help people slow down, ditch the rat race, and get centered. And yes, they do work. Being centered–or grounded–leads to positive emotions, which leads to positive results. Being grounded in yourself and centered in your emotions gives you clarity of thought, which allows you to work out what's important to you in life and what your beliefs and ideals are.

Knowing what you stand for allows you to have confidence, to love yourself, and to believe in yourself. It may seem too simple, but it really is that simple. If you love and believe in yourself as a good person, you will always interact with others on a loving level. This will raise your energetic vibration, allowing you to connect to others on a deeper level and draw abundance into your life.

Now, I say "it's that simple," and the formula IS that simple, but that doesn't mean that putting the formula into action is easy. It isn't easy to make the shift to being a positive person all the time. It takes work, dedication, and more than just mindset. It takes releasing all your anger, your envy, your frustration, your hatred, and all the negative emotions that you feel on a daily basis.

"How do you do that," you ask? You do that through healing. This is where all the exercises you completed in Chapters 4 and 5 come in handy. They have guided you through forgiving yourself and others, getting past your circumstances, and letting go of old pain and hurt so that love and joy can replace them.

In Chapter 4, we began working on your history and pain, how it got there, and why. We also went over a few techniques for releasing that pain. But there is an even deeper way to access the pain you hold inside, and it is through accessing your wounded inner child. This is how you can truly release your past–that foundation of yourself–and rewrite your story to be what you want it to be, not what other people told you it needed to be.

Exercise Eight: Accessing Your Wounded Inner Child
(No Lightning Version)

To access your wounded inner child, you must close your eyes and think back to your earliest memories of yourself as a child. Take this exercise very slowly and allow yourself to really delve deeply into your past. Let your mind take you back to when life was just beginning for you. You may need to practice your meditation or tapping before this becomes doable. It will not be easy for everyone to access their wounded inner child. Let's give it a shot though!

Count backwards from 10 to 1 and visualize a number or age in your mind's eye. This will then present an image or a scene out of your life that should be your first experience with pain, fear, or anger. This is much easier to do and more effective with assistance, but that is not always the case, and it is not always an option for some people. If you find it impossible to do, please don't feel like a failure, you may need assistance and that is absolutely normal.

Below are some questions you can ask yourself to get started. They are designed to help you navigate your memories and find your way back to the part of your childhood that you need to focus on. This is also the exercise that will allow you to further address the deeper pain that may have been attached to the initial pain you addressed in Chapter 4, Exercise One.

1. How was your childhood? Were you happy, sad, indifferent, angry, or unhappy?

2. Did you have a great childhood or one that lacked in love or basic needs?

3. At what age did you "feel" this difference in your life? When did this lack of happiness and joy become blatantly evident when compared to your friends' lives? The age at which you began to notice this difference is the age you want to pinpoint for this exercise.

Find that earliest memory that stands out in your mind after asking yourself these questions, and gently access it. Go and find your child self and ask her (or him) if she has a message for you. Whatever the first thought is that comes to mind IS the message you've asked for. Embrace that message. It may seem insignificant, odd, or even wrong, but it *is* the message that is meant for you at this time. You may need to analyze it and read between the lines to find the meaning of it. You may also want to journal about this experience to help you resolve how the message you received can apply to your life right now.

Now, after the child gives you the message, you need to give your wounded inner child a message in return. Your message should be positive and loving, wholly accepting of the child as they grow. Something like, *"You are perfect as you are, loved, and beautiful."* Or, *"I love you and you are essential to my life."* Or, *"You are everything I need. I love and accept you as you are."* You can adjust the message to be what you know the wounded inner child inside of your adult self still needs to hear. This is also where you remind yourself that all of your life experiences have shaped you into the horse-loving person you are today.

Exercise Nine:
"The Releasing Bubble" Meditation
(No Lightning Version)

Now that you have discovered the pain of your childhood and received the message meant for you, you must enter the Releasing Bubble. The Releasing Bubble is the next step in allowing your negative emotions to dissipate, while leaving a newly recharged space in your soul for all the good thoughts and energy to flow in.

You want to think of your favorite, most relaxing place in the world. It may be next to a lake, listening to the waves at the ocean, sitting on top of your favorite mountain, relaxing at your favorite resort or spa, in your own garden, or at a friend's house. It doesn't matter where it is as long as you feel completely relaxed and at peace. Once you decide on your special space, picture yourself inside a beautiful, safe bubble of bright white light. This bubble of light is filled with God's love and safety. Nothing can harm you in there. You are perfectly safe and at ease.

Now that you're in your safe spot, I want you to think of all the emotions that you encountered when you visited your wounded inner child. Allow those emotions to rise to the top of your heart and float freely within your bubble. As those emotions rise, envision them in some way, maybe as words or as pictures, and see them floating around you.

It is time for you to recognize these emotions and painful memories as pieces of you, pieces that may be painful but that shaped you into who you are today. It's no longer necessary for you to hold onto these memories and emotions, and so I want you to love them. Love them like a newborn baby and just keep on loving on them.

Continue to give them love until they no longer feel painful and instead, are appreciated. They will then feel so light and full of love that they will leave your bubble of light and no longer have any hold over you. The memories will simply be memories with no emotion tied to them any longer. This exercise may take several tries before you feel the full release. If you get stuck, I urge you to contact me at Miranda@mirandavelasquez.com.

Once this exercise has been mastered, you will find it much easier to stay positive and hold a positive mindset. Your days will feel lighter and happier as you go about embracing your horse and aligning yourself with the feelings associated with getting back to riding. This Releasing Bubble meditation can be used every day, for any reason. When used frequently, it becomes a very fast and effective exercise for clearing any negative feelings you may have, along with their associated limiting beliefs, fears, or anything else that leaves you feeling less than all-loving.

When it comes to energy and healing, there is one other subject that I feel must be included in this chapter. I could, of course, share so much more about chakras, vibration, nature, and sensitivities, but I think there is one thing that would be even more helpful to you at this point, and that is an understanding of the healing abilities of animals.

The Animal as Healing Helper

Animals are in tune with human energy and can be the best healers for human beings. There is a reason why animals are brought to hospitals to visit the sick, and why there has been a surge in the use of therapy animals, as well. Dogs that can sense seizures and alert their owner before they occur, guide dogs for the blind, and animals that help treat depression, and other emotional disorders.

Why are animals so helpful in the healing process of humans? I think it's because they can read our energy and adapt quickly to it. They can sense if we are happy, sad, depressed, or in love. They have no human preference or judgment, and their purpose in life is to serve their humans with loyalty and love. There couldn't be a more perfect match for human healing.

Horses, dogs, cats, and so many other animals can be used in your healing process, but remember that if you do not have time to care for an animal properly you should just borrow someone else's. My best and most healing experiences have often happened through a friend's dog or horse. They seem to be ready to give you their love more easily, and know exactly what you need. It may be due to the lack of familiarity that allows the animal to more quickly assess what a stranger needs. The animal's senses are heightened at that initial meeting, trying to sense whether that human is friend or foe.

My favorite animals to work alongside of for healing sessions are horses. They don't possess any ability to judge, and they act like a mirror for human emotions. They really are the most remarkable animals. Whatever emotions you hold within you, they will sense and act accordingly. If you are afraid of them, they will run away. If you are angry, they will back away or refuse to interact with you altogether until your emotions become peaceful. They offer an easy way to recognize what emotions you hold within yourself and then help you to release those emotions and move forward.

The beauty of the horse is that they can naturally help you move toward releasing all your discomforts, until you no longer hold onto them and instead are aligned and balanced in your life.

Exercise Ten:
The Heart Map
(No Lightning Version)

If you're not sure which releasing technique is right for you to use, or if you're looking for a quick exercise for daily use, this is a good one right here: The Heart Map. It's especially good to use as a daily ritual during the hardest times of your healing journey.

To complete the Heart Map exercise, the first step is to draw a big heart onto a piece of paper, then divide your heart drawing into four quadrants. Those four quadrants are labeled "heart," "mind," "body," and "soul." Now, close your eyes and pay extra close attention to each of the corresponding areas inside yourself.

First your heart: what emotions are being held there? Write them down and go on to the next quadrant.

The mind: what negative thoughts are in your mind, sabotaging you today? Write those down and go on to the third quadrant.

The body: what aches, pains, tensions or illnesses are present in your body today? They will be associated with events that are occurring, and/or your current lifestyle.

Lastly, visit with your soul: what intuitions, emotions, and energy do you feel within your soul? Write them down in the final quadrant, as well.

The final step is to review the four quadrants of your Heart Map, and allow yourself to make peace with where you're at in each of these four areas. Recognize their importance, change your actions as necessary to eliminate any negative side effects, and allow them to dissipate from your body. You can burn or shred your Heart Map when the exercise is complete, if you feel it will help you to release any negativity and move forward.

Barn Action

Depending on how far you got last week, I'd like you to try walking forward with your horse this week. If your fear is strong, ask someone to walk you or pony you as you rebuild your confidence. Make sure to take a moment to relax before you mount your horse. Take deep breaths, envision a very beautiful and successful ride, and know that you have been doing the deep work required to release your fears, and that now you are in a place to achieve your dreams.

*Reminder: Practice your weekly joy thoughts every day!

Wisdom from Paris

The biggest thing I notice about humans is that they're always wearing blankets and shoes. They even put blankets and shoes on us horses! Those things just make it harder for me to connect to the earth's energy.

I had to wear a blanket and shoes for awhile, and I was so much happier when they were gone. The blanket was okay, but the shoes were so heavy, I had to lift my feet up really high to trot and canter. That was just too weird. I like naked better.

Chapter 9: Counting on Your Intuitive Confidence

"The intuitive mind is a sacred gift and the rational mind is a faithful servant. We have created a society that honors the servant and has forgotten the gift."

~Albert Einstein

After finding your wounded inner child and releasing your history, you may be feeling a little empty, or even a little bit lost. Sometimes, when the pain you hold inside yourself takes up a lot of space and energy, once you begin to release it, it's like you don't know what to do with yourself. You may be feeling a little out of sorts, and that's totally normal. That occupied space is now free to hold wonderful and positive thoughts and beliefs.

So now, we need to make sure that only positive things take the place that your released negativity once held. Be ready to work during these next two chapters, because this is where you'll really start to shine and feel different.

Since that space inside you is now free to be filled with good stuff, let's make that good stuff all about you. We want to fill it with good stuff about you because your sense of self-worth is going to be a key component to the future success you find in your life. It's time to get really happy and full of self-love.

Self-love doesn't mean ego, and it doesn't mean vanity. It means knowing your value and what you stand for. There's an old adage: *"If you don't stand for something, you'll fall for anything."* If you don't know yourself, you'll be easily manipulated and controlled by anyone and everyone around you. You MUST know yourself, and stand up for your convictions. I find that to be the absolute truth. If you don't know yourself, how are you going to be confident in your horse's eyes? You must be the expert on *you*, because if you can't be the expert on yourself, who can be?

This is where the work to become full of self-love begins. The first exercise you are going to do in this chapter is called "Mirror Work." Mirror Work is the brainchild of author and healer, Louise Hay. I give her *all* the credit for this wonderful and effective exercise.

My clients get amazing results from using Mirror Work, and I do, too. The mirror reflects back to you your thoughts and feelings, and makes it abundantly clear as to where you have resistance or are holding back. It is exceptional how you can truly "see" your feelings when you say them in front of the mirror. You simply cannot hide from your own reflection, and if you feel anything other than confident, you'll find yourself hard to look at.

Most people will tell you to write down your affirmations, and while that *can* be helpful and powerful, I find that doing them along with Mirror Work is even more powerful. This is why I want you to do this exercise for three whole weeks, after which you can go back to writing out your affirmations, if you prefer. Remember, you can always come back to your Mirror Work, too. It will always work for you.

Exercise Eleven:
Mirror Work
(No Lightning Version)

The first thing you want to do is find a mirror in your home and stand in front of it. You are going to look yourself directly in the eyes and get comfortable there. If you can't look yourself in the eyes, you need to go back to the Wounded Inner Child exercise, and do more work there. It's likely that you still have unresolved history that needs clearing before you're able to look yourself in the eyes freely.

Once you're comfortable looking into your gorgeous soulful eyes, we can move on...

Week One

During Week One, while looking deep into your eyes, I want you to say to yourself:

"Insert your name here, I love you.

I really, really love you."

Yes, it feels awkward, but eventually you get used to it.

You might want to invest in a small compact mirror for your bag or office drawer, because you will need to practice this exercise 5 times a day for a week. Do it when you have your restroom break, lunch break, or whatever. You can tell people what you're doing and get them onboard, or whisper to yourself quietly and keep it as a special, secret gift you're giving just to yourself.

Make no mistake, this *is* a gift you're giving yourself. It's not punishment or some weird activity designed to embarrass you; it is a gift. Remember that and thank yourself regularly.

Week Two

Week Two will be a little different. Now that you're comfortable gazing into your eyes and feeling pretty darn loving, you're going to continue with another positive affirmation this week. You are going to look into your eyes and say,

> *"I am unlimited in my potential and I allow (fill in the blank) to flow freely to me."*

You can insert whatever word feels good to you: abundance, love, success, prosperity, etc. Whatever you most desire to have the Universe flow towards you, insert that word into your affirmation. And remember, you want to see your emotions in your own eyes and notice the feelings that your affirmation evokes.

Week Three

Week Three is the time for you to come up with an affirmation for yourself. You can use the affirmations you created in Exercise Seven, or it can even be just a simple statement like, *"This is fun, isn't it?"* Or, *"This horse brings me so much joy."* If you are having a bad day, you can say to yourself, *"It's okay. It's just an obstacle I've had to overcome today. Tomorrow will be better."* Or *"We sure handled the day well even though it was less than perfect."*

The idea is to get you talking to yourself in the mirror. You may feel a little crazy, but again, the mirror reflects your true feelings back to you. You 're learning how to *feel* when something is wrong, when you need to revisit your inner child, when you need to release your fears or negative thoughts, and when you just need to love yourself. This is the beauty of Mirror Work.

Intuition

Now that you have taken three weeks to complete the exercise on Mirror Work, I'll bet you're feeling pretty in tune with yourself... which means that now is the perfect time to discuss intuition.

Intuition is the feeling you get inside your body when you just *know* something. You may know it's going to rain or that your friend is going to show up late. You may have a feeling that someone is lying to you or that the person you just met is going to be your friend forever. No matter what it is, your intuition is something that you should always trust. It will never steer you wrong. In fact, I've had so many clients say that they have consciously made a decision *not* to trust their intuition in one instance or another and immediately regretted it.

Your intuition is your body's BS meter, North Star, and compass. I think of my intuition as God's voice within me, and I'm pretty sure He'd like it if you listen to your intuition, too.

Your intuition will guide you on your path in ways that you can't even imagine, but using it can be confusing sometimes. You have to get comfortable using your instincts *without* second-guessing them. That's where it gets confusing, when you find yourself questioning it: Is that my intuition? What if it's wrong? What if that's my brain just interfering? How do I know it's my intuition?

If your mind starts spinning with questions, remind yourself to breathe and relax. Yes, it's your intuition. Yes, your brain will be interfering. As for the rest of those questions, the answer is always TRUST. Trust yourself. Trust in God and the Universe, and trust in Jesus (or whoever it is you believe in.)

Have you ever taken a multiple-choice test and when you went back over your answers, you notice that you had made some changes because you didn't trust your first response, finding out later that your first answer was correct? Frustrating, right? Don't do that to your life. Your intuition is responsible for that first answer that pops into your mind, so just trust your first answer and trust your intuition.

Once you begin to trust your intuition, it gets easier and better. It becomes your go-to source for gauging what is right and wrong, which is another beautiful gift you give to yourself. You will use it to connect to the Divine, His angels and Jesus. You will begin to use it to monitor your own well-being. You'll instinctively know when you need to provide yourself with rest and relaxation, or when you need to end the party, or when you need to get into nature and detox. You will most certainly use it to read your horse's body language and energy. It will help you immensely when connecting with both yourself and your horse. Intuition is abundantly powerful and a gift that keeps on giving.

You will use it outside the horse pen as well, when you make the decision of which job you will choose, or what direction you want to take in your life. It is what you will use as a parent when you care for your children, and it is what you will fall back on when you feel threatened. The more you use your intuition, the more honed it will become, making it a very powerful tool in your life, and as crucial as any of your other senses.

My story is a perfect example of why it's so important to hone your intuition. I had a few years where I was *not* using mine at all. It led me to marry the wrong man and stay too long in that unhealthy relationship, only to finally be cheated on and divorced. But once I started using my intuition again, I immediately found the sweetest, most supportive partner. One who is generous and kind. I became step-mom to a beautiful teenage girl, my young boys continued to flourish, I found a wonderful horse-boarding facility, and I had my little miracle daughter who came to me after my own healing journey, despite genetic abnormalities that run in my family and my being over 40. She truly is a miracle and was blessed by Jesus while in my womb. (That is a story in and of itself, and the most powerful experience of love I have ever felt in my life.) Oh, and the owners of that horse-boarding facility... they've since become my daughter's Godparents. Using my intuition has gained me everything and lost me nothing. If you're afraid of your intuition for some reason, I urge you not to be. It is glorious.

Now before we move on, I want to leave you with one final suggestion. Being in a state of health and well-being will help your intuition work more effectively, especially while you're in the process of honing it. If you do not take care of yourself, your intuition will be stunted. You must have proper nutrition, exercise, and sleep. If you feel out of sync, you should listen to your body and slow down, take a camping trip, go to the spa, or take a walk. Caring for yourself allows you to be fully present in your life, to appreciate it, and to relish your personal journey. What a beautiful feeling, and what a beautiful foundation you will have to continue connecting with your horse and the rest of the Universe.

*Reminder: Practice your weekly joy thoughts every day!

Wisdom from Paris

The best thing to do when you're afraid is to trust your intuition. Fear makes everything feel uncertain and it's easy to become blinded by it. If you use and trust your intuition every day, like horses do, then you'll know which path to take, even if fear is trying to undermine you.

Chapter 10: Trusting the Divine and Finding Your Balance

"What in your life is calling you? When all the noise is silenced, the meetings adjourned, the lists laid aside, and the wild iris blooms by itself in the dark forest, what still pulls on your soul? In the silence between your heartbeats hides a summons, do you hear it? Name it, if you must, or leave it forever nameless, but why pretend it is not there?"

~ *The Terma Collective*

Balance

People are too often hyper-focused on themselves. We worry about our careers, our families, our money, and our horses. We tend to set aside our need to give back, to serve others, and to connect to our deeper selves and to Source.

When you become so focused on your personal life that you forget about your friends and family, or about having fun, that's when you build up your stress levels and inadvertently cause pain to the people and animals around you. You end up creating a toxic environment for your family and yourself. It's really easy to get caught up in wanting to be successful, wanting to grow your career, or wanting to provide for your family...and it's not *wrong*; it's just not balanced.

Work can often be the culprit behind many of your fears and worries. Will you be employed next week? Do you have enough money? How will you make it work? It is not conducive to anyone's lifestyle to be overburdened and stressed out by work *or* life. It will destroy your relationship with your horse and with your family.

It is extremely important for you to have balance in your life, to care for yourself as you would care for your child or your mother. Without gentle treatment of yourself, you will burn out, become ill-tempered, or even bitter. No one wants to be around someone like that, and no one wants to feel like that either, so balance yourself and you won't have to worry about it.

How do you go about ensuring you're a balanced person? Do a quick self-check every day and see how you're feeling. It's pretty easy to do: simply ask yourself how you're feeling and pay attention to those feelings within your body (like we did in Exercise 6).

For instance, you may feel that you don't want to go into work today; honor that feeling. Don't listen to your brain saying that you HAVE to and NEED to, just ask yourself if you WANT to. Yes, there will always be days that you can't reschedule, but you also need to recognize that you are more productive when you are healthy.

Staying balanced and grounded means you will have less sick days, too. We all know how nice it is to rarely get sick...and if that isn't your experience, you need to really consider your situation carefully. Self-care will drastically change your health and wellness. How you treat your body will start a chain reaction. Eat well, exercise, drink lots of water, and get good sleep and you will be a naturally healthier person that gets sick less.

The same is true of your emotional system; if you check in with yourself, have fun, love big, express your feelings in a healthy way, and take "Me" days, you'll be happier, wealthier and wiser. Why? Because a happier person is more likely to make more money, ride their horse more often, be full of gratitude, and have an optimally functioning brain, as well.

If you think your self-care could be better, your first step is to set boundaries. You need to establish boundaries with your friends, family, colleagues, and with yourself. Start with scheduling a day off. Pick a day, schedule it, plan something really fun and tempting to do, and then take the day off.

Don't let anyone fool you into thinking you don't deserve it; EVERYONE deserves time off. Don't think that your office, colleagues, business associates, clients, or even your children can't survive without you. The world will not stop if you are unavailable for 24 hours. Your body and mind will surely thank you, though.

If it's a family self-care day, I'm sure that your children and/or spouse will appreciate spending some quality time with you...and if it's just a "Me" day, that's even better! Do something that you love to do or something that makes you feel great. That thing will be different for everyone: take a trail ride, go wine tasting, take a hike or go to the spa. Whatever you choose, it should feel like a refuge from the world.

When you rest your soul, it will rejuvenate your entire system. And if you take time for yourself, you will be a better rider who is better able to connect with your horse. You'll also find that your horse is more attuned to your energy. So take some "horse" time for yourself and it just might help you get back to riding sooner rather than later.

Spirituality

***"To understand the soul of a horse is the closest human beings can come to knowing perfection." ~* Author Unknown**

Now, not everyone who reads this book is going to be spiritual, but I do still want to talk to you about really getting connected to God, Source, Mother Nature, or whatever you may call your higher power. I will use God because that's who I believe in, but feel free to use whatever title you prefer.

Connecting to God or a power greater than you is so important. It is important because it will make a difference in the way you live your life. It offers you hope, and leads your thoughts towards an afterlife, heaven, or reincarnation. It helps disperse the feelings of a finite life and lends itself to the thoughts of life after death. It helps keep you on the right side of the law, and it keeps you loving big and connecting to nature.

I talked about how we are all energy in Chapter 8, and about how everything around us is energy, as well. There are some people that can see and read that energy, and others that have other "gifts." The fact that we are all made up of atoms of energy is scientifically proven and it does not mean that God did not create us. In fact, the way it is described is that when looked at microscopically, all energy is created from fractals.

Now I'm not a scientist, but I do have an education in a scientific field and I have done a lot of research. What I know is that fractals are never-ending patterns. They are infinitely complex and self-similar across varying sizes. They are the same image repeated over and over, occurring on both miniscule and larger scales all across nature. The rivers, the oceans, and the mountains are all made up of fractals. Fractals are cross-dimensional as well. How can that not be a verification of a higher power? I know that's heavy and a bit beyond riding horses, but I think it's really important to be curious and continue to learn as long as life will let you.

The Horse-Human Connection

"Wherever man has left his footprints in the long ascent from barbarism to civilization, we find the hoofprint of a horse beside it."
~ **John Trotwood Moore**

Look at the horse. How could it be possible that such a majestic and strong beast not be a miracle of God? A horse is a prey animal and humans are predators, yet our connection to each other and our ability to trust each other and work together is magical. It feels mythical and ancient. It blows my mind every day that a gentle-natured prey animal would allow a human to put a rope upon his face, a saddle on his back, and give almost full control of his body over to that human.

The connection between horses and humans runs so deep into history that it's as if we have horse blood in our veins, or that our instincts were made to work together. We can clearly communicate with each other through our energy fields and intuitive senses. If we take the time to get to know each other we can read each other perfectly. I don't think there is a more magical human-animal bond in our Universe.

To ride a horse is the ultimate blessing from nature. I almost feel as if the gift of the horse to man is a reassurance that mankind is good enough to accept such a wondrous companion. To be in such close proximity with a naturally wild beast is a testament to the good within man. As you know, if the horse feels an evil around it, it will flee. So take heart that no matter what you think, say or do, you are inherently good, kind and loving. Just look to your horse for proof of that.

The reason I bring this up is because it is important to realize that you are part of something bigger. You DO have the support of the Universe, and God, and all of God's instruments. You can rely on Him to be your provider and protector. You can ask for what you need and expect it to be given to you when He is ready to, of course... Although, there are certain ways of making sure that you are not resisting and repelling what He wants to give you, and that is through releasing any negative thoughts or trauma and allowing yourself to be open to receiving His gifts.

Connecting to God through nature, horses, and love will always regenerate your emotional and physical body. It will become a big part of the way you balance your life. By asking for support from God on your epic journey of change, and allowing yourself to shift into what you *feel* instead of what you *think* you should be, you're freeing yourself from those fears. Things will be easier as you continue to trust in the

Universe and relish the path that has been placed in front of you.

Exercise Twelve:
Studying Your Horse's Behavior
(No Lightning Version)

Every time you go to the barn, I ask that you use your journal and take notes of your interactions with your horse. Read your horse's energy, jot down how his behavior was that day, how you connected or didn't connect with him, and learn his body language.

Study him in his herd and learn their ways, too. You can watch the herd to discover who is the leader, where your horse belongs in the hierarchy and how they interact with each other. This will help you to understand what your horse is used to and what he expects from you.

Write down everything you find and make sure you put the date at the top of each journal entry. This will serve as an historical account of the beautiful growth in your relationship. There is nothing more beautiful than deeply knowing the animal that is giving over their control to you.

Taking these notes will also serve as a horse health and behavior journal, and can help if any problems were to arise.

Now that we have covered spirituality, I'd like to acknowledge that some of you might be looking for more information on how to become spiritual. If you *are* looking for more information, I suggest you go to the library and read some books on spirituality that interest you. If you are looking to learn more about a particular religion, attending one of their church meetings will be informative and most likely inspiring.

If you don't feel comfortable with either of those options, you can perhaps ask someone you know that is already a spiritual person. They might be able to provide information and/or guidance, and will most likely be happy to help in some capacity.

Of course, there is always the option of working with me directly! If that option is the most appealing or exciting, you can contact me at dreamwestfarm@gmail.com.

*Reminder: Practice your weekly joy thoughts every day!

Wisdom from Paris

After a good rain, when the sun begins to shine down and warm the earth, I like to lie down and feel that warmth and the energy of my ancestors flood into my skin.

Chapter 11: Is Your Relationship with Your Horse Strong Enough?

"At its finest, rider and horse are joined not by tack, but by trust. Each is totally reliant upon the other. Each is the selfless guardian of the other's very well-being."

~ Unknown

Over the course of this book so far, we have addressed how to recognize, release, and move past your fears. You have worked on yourself, learned to love yourself, and found your confidence. Now it's time to address how you show up for your horse, how you define your relationship with your horse, and why I have waited until Chapter 11 to finally talk about this.

I waited because without you being emotionally healthy, brave, and less fearful, it might have been detrimental to both you and your horse to bring it up earlier. Your attention would have been split between trying to strengthen your connection to your horse while also attempting to let go of your fears at the same time; that's just too dang hard. You need to take it one step at a time for the CONNECTING program to work. Let's finally apply what you've learned to help you show up for your horse.

There are many horses and horse riders all around the world, and we all treat our horses differently. Some differences are due to cultural preferences, some are due to regional geographies, affordability, availability, and societal opinions. You may choose to house your horse in a barn, ride in large competitive events, pull his mane, trace clip him, or keep a light in his stall. Others may keep their horse in their backyard, ride him around the neighborhood and let his whiskers and hair grow long. No matter what you choose, the choice is yours. If you are reading this book, I know something about you and your horse, and it's something that everyone reading this book has in common: you want to build a deeper connection to your horse.

The easiest, best, and most obvious way to do that is to spend time with your horse. You don't have to ride, just be. Be there together, breathing in the same scent of hay and manure while you assess each other's energy. Energy is such an important thing to comprehend. I touched on it earlier: we are all atoms, atoms are energy, and therefore we are all energy.

Everything around us is energy, even solid and inanimate objects; things like furniture are comprised of atoms and energy. That being said, we ALL have the capability to read each other's energy. You may not be attuned to it at first, but if you earnestly pay attention and open yourself up to it, it will come. It's not magical, although it feels like it sometimes. It's just where science and spirituality intersect.

Reading your horse's energy comes initially through learning his body language. Everyone knows that if the ears pin back flat against a horse's head it means that he's angry and you'd better get out of the way. A horse's ears have their own language and they're fun to watch as they swivel around.

If you really want a deeper connection to your horse, allow him to *be* a horse. Put him in pasture with a few other horses and watch the herd develop. Where does your horse fit in? Is he the "head mare," the middle guy, or the low man on the totem pole? This is important to know because it will teach you how your horse expects YOU to behave.

If he *is* low man, he needs you to support him, lead him, and be the boss. Get after him when he oversteps his bounds and keep him in his place. I'm not saying to mistreat him, just assert yourself. That's not being mean, that's how a herd behaves and you are speaking horse.

If you don't set the tone for your relationship, your horse will, and that won't be good. If you allow your horse to be the "head mare" in your relationship, he will put you in *your* place. He will nip you, push you, disrespect your personal space, and walk all over you. That is not safe for either of you.

If you don't have any experience with putting your horse to pasture, watching him in the herd, or asserting yourself, please find a natural horsemanship facilitator whom you respect, and learn from them. Without this necessary experience, you might end up creating other problems, or getting seriously hurt.

Another thing to be aware of is which other horse, or horses, your horse connects to. If he doesn't get along with a particular horse, don't put him next to that horse anymore; it's making him uncomfortable and his focus won't be on you. And if your horse's focus is not on you, he will be in a state of fear.

Horses operate in a range of emotions: one is fear, another is playfulness, and a third is relaxed. You want your horse to be relaxed, not fearful or playful, unless you dictate otherwise. There will be circumstances in which you'll need to assert that your horse changes their emotional state to fearful or playful, but if your horse doesn't see *you* as his leader, he won't listen to you when you do.

Another great way to connect with your horse is to do liberty work. Groundwork is effective as well, but you may get more satisfaction and a deeper bond from doing liberty work. When your horse is at liberty it means that they are free of all tack and working with you of their own accord. If you're interested in trying this technique, there are several great tutorials available on YouTube for simple liberty activities to do with your horse.

The reason liberty work creates a stronger bond between you and your horse is because the horse is *choosing* to do this work. He is liberated from all encumbrances, and he is free to trust you, as you are to trust him. When you play together in this fashion it creates a "best friend" relationship, kind of like when you were a child making friends with the other kids. Play equals enjoyment, and enjoyment equals good memories that everyone wants more of, your horse included.

The next tool I want to discuss is grooming. Grooming is how horses connect to each other. They nip and chew on each other's withers and rub their faces on each other's bodies as a form of affection. Grooming your horse tells him that he is loved and that you enjoy his company.

Why is it important that he *knows* you enjoy his company? Because you want mutual admiration to be the goal. No one is happy when you're confused with just another feed bucket. When you groom your horse, you also have the ability to look over his body condition, find his itchy spots and learn what relaxes him.

Another thing you can do during grooming is apply essential oils to your horse, or allow him to smell them. Aromatherapy and scent have such a strong tie to memory and emotion that both you and your horse will associate the scent of your chosen oils with a blissfully relaxing and bonding experience. Every time your horse smells that familiar scent, like lavender for example, he will think of you and what a great time you always have together. There are so many ways to bond with your horse, but the ways above are some of the easiest, and produce results rapidly.

But the most important bonding tool you can use with your horse is time. Time is something that humans understand but horses don't. They have a routine that occurs by the light of the sun or the moon, but they do not keep time. They know when it's feeding time or turnout time, but those are just kept by the sun. Humans use time to schedule out our days and to include more in them. We use time to push ourselves to the limit and then try to "find the time" to relax.

What horses know is that either you are there or you are not. They like it when you are there, feeding them, grooming them, walking with them and just BEING with them. Take the time to be a member of your horse's herd, stand next to him while he grazes, and massage his withers.

We often try to push our schedules onto our horses, limiting the time we have for them. Yet still we expect the horse to cooperate with that half-hour we've allotted to give him his bath.

That's not going to happen. Your horse is going to read your energy–which basically means he's going to read your mind–and then he's going to rebel like a teenager...because as soon as there is a time limit, that horse will push it till it's completely broken.

But if you have given time to your horse and you still are not connecting with him, you may need to reassess both your and your horse's ability to connect. It might mean that one of you simply is incapable of connecting...but that doesn't necessarily mean it's the end.

Yes, it might mean that the two of you are not meant for each other, but it could also just mean that more work needs to be done. Don't give up too easily. Try the suggestions I mentioned in this chapter and spend time with your horse for 60 full days. If you haven't bonded after 60 days of grooming, grazing, liberty work, treats and herd-watching time, that's when it's time to consider parting ways...but not before.

You should be with your horse at least two hours a day, three days a week in order to cultivate this connection. If you can do more, that's even better, but if that's not possible, you can still see results by spending a minimum of 6 hours per week with your horse.

But...sometimes you *do* have to ask yourself:

"Is this the right horse for me?"
"Should I be riding this horse?"
"How do I feel about riding this horse?"
"Do I love him?"

Yes, I said, "Do I love him?" Love may sound ridiculous to some of you reading this. To others, it may sound like the most natural thing in the world. But, if you can't find enough love in your heart for your horse, how are you going to care enough to connect deeply with him, get into his emotional energy field, and ride him again with ease?

Think about all the horses you've ridden, the horses you've bonded with and had a deeper connection with. You probably have a special place in your heart for your favorites versus all the others. My motto is this: if you don't love that horse and you don't want to ride him, then allow your horse to find a human partner that they *will* love and connect with. If you don't, it will always be a poor-to-moderate experience for both your horse and for you as the rider.

I'm sure you'd much rather have an excellent relationship with your horse. Doesn't everyone want excellent relationships? I know your horse would rather be loved than loathed. There is no shame in recognizing that the horse you own does not suit you because you just don't have a connection. It is a crucial step towards understanding your deeper self, and knowing what is right for you.

I want to reiterate here that there is no shame or guilt in allowing yourself to release a horse from your ownership. Think about what's best for you and your horse. Is it to stay together and tough it out to find that lost connection? Sometimes humans drift apart or get a divorce, and we're the same species, speaking the same language!

Horses and their humans can drift apart as well. Needs can change over time, both yours and those of your horse. Often times we love a horse for it's looks and don't consider the personality. Horse personalities vary as much as human ones do, so making sure that you and your horse get along is super important.

Really take the time to evaluate your situation and do what's best for you both. Sometimes we hold on tight, thinking that no one could give our horse a better home than we could, but the reality just doesn't match up. In those situations, the best thing is to let go. It could turn out to be a really good thing if you rehome your horse and it brings harmony to both of your lives. That's the most important thing to remember.

Barn Action

The ultimate goal of this book is to reconnect you with your horse and help you release any fears you may have surrounding them. This week, I would like you to take the time to reassess your relationship with your horse.

Go to your horse, spend time with him, watch his body language, and see what you become aware of. Touch him all over and pick up his feet. You can even try to ride, if you feel up to it.

When you have done that, really think long and hard about how your relationship has changed. Are your fears still there? Do you feel bonded to your horse in a deeper way than before you read this book? Make a note of any changes you see and things you may need to keep working on. Feel inside your body and really listen to yourself.

If you notice that there are things that need more attention, write them down and work on them. Our horses deserve our best, so let's give it to them.

*Reminder: Practice your weekly joy thoughts every day!

Wisdom from Paris

People that visit me aren't always there, present in the moment. I see them staring off into space and I wonder where they are, and what they're thinking. I know they're not with me and I wonder how they got that way, and when they'll come back.

Chapter 12: Notes for Those with Disabilities, Competitive Riders, and How to Connect with Other People's Horses

"Champions do not become champions when they win the event, but in the hours, weeks, months, and years they spend preparing for it. The victorious performance itself is merely the demonstration of their champion character."

~T. Alan Armstrong

Disabilities

Our population is continually changing and growing in diversity. We are learning new ways to include all types of people in all sorts of activities that were not possible in the recent past. People are now able to hike using prosthetic legs, or barrel race like Amberley Snyder, even though they are paraplegic. (She's so brave!) They can ski down mountains through adaptive ski programs, or play wheelchair basketball and compete in the Special Olympics.

There are many people out there who are newly discovering how working with horses can help with their disabilities. For some, that may be through "Hippotherapy," also known as Horseback Riding Therapy. Hippotherapy is often used as a means to help people access and strengthen muscles that they don't normally use. It creates new neural pathways in the brain and strengthens coordination for people who don't have a full range of motion, or are not able to exercise in more traditional ways. It can also help with sensory issues, such as deficiencies in the vestibular sense, proprioception, and overall balance.

I've personally seen the benefits of this sort of therapy in action. My non-verbal sister used Hippotherapy many years ago to help her strengthen her muscles and improve her ability to walk. But she gained much more than just the strength that she would have in any physical therapy session. She also connected with her therapy horses, enjoyed their company, and truly loved every second of her time with them. It was a delight for everyone in my family to see the joy on her face when she was with them, even if she had no words to speak it aloud.

Today, there are even more varieties of equine healing available for those interested in the healing power of horses. Besides the therapeutic riding I mentioned above, new techniques include, Equine Guided Education, Equine-Assisted Psychotherapy, and Equine-Facilitated Learning experiences.

Equine Guided Education was created by Ariana Strozzi, and focuses on somatics, intuition, and life purpose. Equine-Assisted Psychotherapy is beneficial for those who may need the assistance of a licensed counselor. And my certification with the HERD Institute is in Equine-Facilitated Learning, which is more experiential, focusing on what the individual experiences when in the presence of the horse.

There are even more types of equine healing available than the ones I've listed above, and each one will appeal to a different individual. Most of these equine-guided therapeutic programs fall under the purview of governing bodies, but some are not governed.

What I want to make clear, though, is that I am *not* an authority on assisting those with disabilities to get back on a horse, nor do I offer therapeutic interventions on the subject. Each person has their own individual needs, far more than I could ever address in this single book. What I *can* say is that the exercises I have laid out in the book are similar to those that have been recommended to me by licensed counselors. Following them can help manage your anxiety and fears, both when mounted and unmounted.

However, for those who have more advanced physical disabilities or mental health disorders, these exercises do not replace the need for professional help. Please, if you have disabilities that prevent you from riding without assistance, find a licensed professional that can help you. Your safety is most important.

I'll leave it to you to decide which, if any, of these therapeutic methods you'd like to explore further. Just remember that when seeking out an equine healing modality, the horses are not tools, they are the teachers.

Competing on Your Horse or Someone Else's

Finding a way to love and connect with your *own* horse is hard enough, so what happens when you are a competitive rider and you need to connect to other people's horses? Well, it *can* be hard if you let it be...or this chapter can help you make it much easier.

Some of you may find it easier to connect to other people's horses because you don't know their every nuance and bad habit. You just see what they show you, and that may be different from what they show their owner.

The easiest way to connect with someone else's horse is to allow yourself to see them as clients that you are meant to serve. These horse-clients were sent from God in order for you to connect with them for some specific reason. You may only have a few precious moments to make an impression on that horse, but that may be all that is needed.

You may have been sent this horse to help them in some way. You may be meant to serve them by showing them what a beautiful thing a horse/human bond can be, and to support them through a stage of their growth. We all know growth can happen with one realization in just a split second, so always be prepared to be positive and supportive with your client's or your own competitive horses.

If you are finding that you and your mount are no longer working together as a team, or winning your events, you may have lost your connection. Maybe you have fear around a specific mount, or around riding in general.

Did you have a negative experience? Has it left you all too aware of how badly it can hurt if you fall off the horse? If you have answered "yes" to any of the above, you need to go back to Chapter 4 and work through these particular horse-related fears, recognizing and embracing them so that they can be released.

As you work through each chapter, let forgiveness be your goal. A horse is a horse. They each may have a different job, but they are still a horse...just like you are still just a human, no matter what job you have. You react to situations, have preferences and various moods. Horses do, too. Don't forget to allow your mount to be a horse and allow yourself to be a human.

Neither one of you is perfect but you can still be special together.

You may never know the reason you've been put into contact with a particular horse, so I say make the absolute best of it. It may be that you need the help of that horse to push past your fear of going just a little faster, or just a little higher. The horse is, more often than not, the teacher.

You'll always learn new things from every horse you ride or connect with, but there will be certain horses that teach you something really special. One horse may come into your life to show you how great it can be to work together as a team. Another may be sent to you to teach you patience.

Each horse will take you on a journey, and you can either embrace that journey or fight it. If you're feeling fear around riding, you're probably fighting your journey right now. Try to relax, embrace your fears, realize that they are natural and normal, and then release them. Being a competitive rider will always have its ups and downs, wins and losses, but if you make a special effort to connect to the horse you ride, you'll enjoy every minute of it.

I can't give you the perfect formula for winning, but if you follow the exercises in this book, you'll be in the best place possible to win because you'll have a healthy mindset, one that is filled with joy and gratitude rather than fear and frustration.

If you're finding it hard to work with a particular horse or client, try to find something to love about them. The key is to find a way to release your judgments so that you can connect with that client's horse.

Oftentimes, the horse has bad habits that are not his fault; proper training just wasn't in place from the beginning. Try to overlook these faults and don't judge. Your job is to help and heal this horse. If you're patient and listening carefully, the horse will whisper his problems and secrets to you.

I heard of one horse that wouldn't canter or lope for anyone. He just flat out refused, so they called in an Equine Communicator. The Communicator told them that the horse wanted to do something different. He didn't like competing and showing, but he really liked ranch work. His owners put him to work on the ranch, and his problems went away.

What does this mean for you? It means that maybe you just need to listen to yourself and listen to the horse. Watch his body language when he's working. If he's resistant and refusing, he may be more suited to a different job. If he's not performing well, maybe he needs a break...and the same goes for you. Burnout is real and you need to watch for that, too. Allow yourself to have fun, relax, and rejuvenate. When you're happy it reflects onto your partners, both horse *and* human.

You may have noticed that when you are eager to ride a horse, the horse is eager to learn. When you approach your competitive mount, the horse sizes you up just like you do to him. When you are in your perfect energetic zone that carries over into the horse's energetic zone, as well.

Happy rider equals happy horse, right? Yes, but as a competitive rider, feelings of fear may be showing up when you compete, as well. It may be when riding your own horse or someone else's horse, and that can create a problem for you. How do you compete on a horse that you've had a traumatic experience with, or one that you're just not connecting with anymore?

The answer is, you either find a way to fix the problem, or you get a different horse. The problem with getting a different horse is that those same fears and struggles may continue to haunt you, following you from horse to horse and destroying your competitive career. Why doesn't the problem just magically fix itself when you get another horse? Because the problem is not the horse, the problem is you.

If you skipped over the first eleven chapters of this book and have started reading at this point, go back and start the book over. The topics relate to you just as much as to any other horse owner or rider. And yes, not connecting to the horse you're riding can sometimes be a problem with the horse, but usually it isn't.

The horse may need some time to get to know you, but if you treat him well, and spend time bonding with him, he'll perform harder and better for you than for anyone else. The trick is in creating that bond. A great bonding tool is food. Horses are food-motivated, as you are well aware of, I'm sure. Bringing them treats can endear you to them.

An even better bonding tool is to take the horse on a grazing walk. Be his herd and stand by him as he eats. He knows you're there and as he drops his head, his relaxation level increases. If he's completely relaxed and enjoying his time with you, he's going to recognize and enjoy your relationship together. This doesn't have to be hours long, though it can be if that's what you prefer. It all depends on you and the horse; even a few minutes can make a tremendous difference in your relationship.

When the horse enjoys his time with you, he looks forward to being with you. He comes when you call him across the field, hugs your neck, and you create a bond.

Love is an essential part of competing, in that it can make you feel loved by family, friends and colleagues, and (if you allow yourself to feel it) even by God. But you have to make the effort to recognize the love that you have in your life and focus on it.

Give hugs frequently and let them linger. Did you know that giving a hug for 30 seconds can have a healing effect? It takes at least 30 seconds for your cells to register the love being received, but then your cells actually change because of that received love. That's how powerful love can be in your life. Embrace it! Hug it out and allow love to reign in your life.

Does that sound sappy? Yes, but it absolutely does work! It's very similar to positive thinking. The more love you bring into your life, the better the horses, the more wins, and the more abundance you'll have.

As a competitive rider, you are oftentimes coaching your clients through their decisions. Should this horse compete at a higher level or should he stay at the lower level? Should you ride client's horse #1 in the show, or horse #2?

When the client can't make the decision, it's the perfect opportunity for you to break out your intuitive skills. What is it about horse #1 that makes you feel he should or shouldn't compete at that level? Will you regret your decision if your horse doesn't participate in that show? Will it really hurt his career if you give or deny him that opportunity?

You can also ask your clients to use their intuition, or teach them how to use it for themselves if they are unsure. It will help them move through their blocks, just like you are doing as you read this book. Tell them to close their eyes and ask themselves which horse they picture winning that buckle or ribbon. The first answer that pops into their mind is the right answer. Don't second-guess it; don't think on it for 5 minutes. Give them 5 seconds to receive their answer and move forward from there.

Do the same thing when you're interviewing clients to be their competitive rider. Ask them what they see their horse being used for, but also allow them the freedom to dream. Ask them, "What is your ideal dream result for yourself and your horse?" Let them think about it and tell you. This will help them become more realistic and grounded in their decisions, and they'll also come to understand the way you work.

Explain to them that not every horse and rider connect well, and that you need to not just ride their horse, but bond with him, as well. Explain that you'll both do better if you have a good relationship, rather than just being strangers. And if you don't feel either love or respect for that horse or that client, then you really should pass on the opportunity, and suggest they look for another rider.

Or, if you find that you just can't release your fears connected to a certain horse, then you should pass that horse along to another rider as well, one who is a better fit for him. We cannot connect with every horse and every client. The goal is to serve those that *are* a good fit and make all parties involved happy and well-satisfied. Excellent service provided and an excellent experience for all involved; that's what you want. Only work with the people who move your world, who make you smile and feel happy.

If you create a respectful client-training system, you'll be getting as many clients as you want. If you use your intuition in your career, you'll see more happy clients and less frustration. Not to mention, you'll be the "go-to" rider for anyone who wants to feel respected and inspired.

Barn Action

Take the time to visit and bond with your client's horses. Show the horses and the client that you care, and that you want to build a relationship with all of them. Walk with the horses, groom the horses, and speak gently to them.

*Reminder: Practice your weekly joy thoughts every day!

Wisdom from Paris

Our horse herd is full of different personalities and different abilities. We can't survive without each other; different is what keeps us alive. Some in our herd are strong and athletic, some are sweet and sensitive, and some are mean and protective. They all have a different job and serve a different purpose.

Chapter 13: Giving Up is NOT an Option!

"You always knew that one day you would stand up...
That you would raise the standard of your life...
That one day you would say to yourself,
"Enough with this bull$h!t..."
You might as well make that day today."

~Steve Maraboli

You may be wondering why I have a chapter titled "Giving Up is NOT an Option!" It's here to remind you that there are always going to be obstacles in your way. It's a hard truth to accept, but a good one to remember. When you are able to remember this, you can recognize obstacles for what they are, and consciously choose how to handle them.

I have provided you with the steps to recognize and release your fears and you are now free to ride off into the sunset with your horse. I have given you the reins and you simply have to choose to lope off. This sounds like a perfect ending, but sometimes it's not that easy.

You'll want to be more considered with your thoughts from here on out. When you are afraid of all the changes inside and around you, what you may be doing is inadvertently calling obstacles onto your path. Unconsciously, that can happen. You'll read this book and think you're definitely going to do all the exercises in it, and maybe you even start to do them, but then you get sick. Think of getting sick as a test. You're sick because God wants to see if you'll really stick through making the changes you say you want to make.

When you're sick, or you get fired, or you hit some sort of emergency or obstacle, it's usually a test. It's much easier to view it as a test as well, rather than dwelling on the idea that you're hitting obstacles because God doesn't want you to succeed. If you think like that you'll never succeed. But, if you believe that you're on the right path, and you feel that God has a plan for you, then He does and you are!

You will face many tests and obstacles on your life's journey, and you will handle them each in a different way, *and* in different ways than others might handle the same situations. Some people handle obstacles with grace and fortitude, while others crumble and fail, rising from the ashes like a phoenix in order to move on. Some people brave their obstacles alone and others need a helping hand. Whichever way you choose to handle your obstacles, remember that it's likely you will feel quite a bit of discomfort and a loss of control. That's the trademark feeling you get when you're going through an epic change like this.

Sidenote: I really don't believe that God picks on us or gives us more than we can bear. If you continue hitting obstacles all the time, return to the beginning of the CONNECTING program, and reassess your mindset, blocks, resistance to accepting His gifts, and your balance, because chances are there is something there that needs some fine-tuning.

Change on a level such as this can be scary, or it can be delightful. It really depends on where you were on your journey before you picked up this book. If you had never thought about your life path, your fears, or done any kind of personal development work before this, then you may be feeling rocked to your core right now. You may not recognize your thoughts or your feelings as they undergo this big shift. Congratulations, you're awakening!

If you *have* done previous personal development work and you recognize all of your feelings, and are excited and happy to expand on them, then you may be in just the right place. Your awareness is expanding and growing, along with your thoughts and feelings, and you're traveling along your life path in a brilliant way.

But, the more important this work is to you, the more resistance you will feel. You'll need to fight for your dreams. Fight through your resistance, and fight for your ability to BE YOU. You will have naysayers, negative thoughts, and people who tell you to just hurry up and get back in the saddle. That's just how life works. You have to understand your resistance in order to move beyond it. If you don't recognize it, you may just quit under the pressure instead of pushing through. But this is the time where you *need* to push through. Don't give up. Stay dedicated and keep moving forward, no matter how small the step may be.

Throughout this book, I taught you how to implement the changes you need to make in order to get back in the saddle, and trust me, I know how hard that can be. Maybe you're thinking, "It was easier for you, Miranda. You're not where I am. MY circumstances are special or different." I *have* been where you are, and I will continue to be where you are over and over again until I meet our Creator.

No matter what your circumstances, the point is, you have to *want* to make this change. I want you to be courageous enough to seek help in making the change if you need it. To get out of your own way so that your mind can process the change. In this way you'll become a steadfast soldier in your commitment to realizing your dreams. You have intuition and you have a voice; use them both to your advantage. Find them, tap into them, and allow them to propel you towards your goals and dreams.

It's not easy to complete this journey, but please don't give up! You may not understand why it's so hard now, but later it'll be clear to you. There is always a journey attached to your life, and you will go through multiple journeys in your lifetime. Each one will have so many lessons for you to learn during your short time on earth. Some souls don't have enough time to complete all their journeys, or learn all their lessons in one lifetime, so they may come back to finish their journey.

I also want you to remember that change is hard, change is uncomfortable, but no growth can occur without change. Just that right there is cause for celebration. The fact that you are reading this right now means that you have taken a step towards making that change. You have gone further than many people ever will. You have stopped complaining, worrying, and analyzing, and have taken a productive step forward.

So many people complain about their lives and say that they are unhappy, but then they do nothing to change their circumstances. Is it because they are cowards or feeble? I don't think so. What I *do* think is that without proper support and accountability, many people have a hard time moving forward. They get so deep into their minds that they forget to get out of their own way. It's also very hard to change one's routine. We are all creatures of habit, and when we try to go against our established routines, it becomes difficult to stick to it. It *can* be done but it's not easy.

As you have probably realized by now, discovering your true fears and changing your routines can be difficult. Asking yourself the hard questions can be helpful, but you may still feel like there is more. More to dig deep for, more to uncover, more to awaken to...and it's true, there probably is.

It's no small task to act as your own facilitator when working through your fears. Just as it's helpful to have someone lead you through discovering your dreams and passions, or your pains and problems, it is often much more cathartic to have someone lead you through uncovering and working through your fears.

Going it alone can take a lot longer than if you have some help. I once watched an interview with a monk who had spent 4 long years in solitude, discovering his ability to be okay with himself, to embrace his discomfort, and to feel his oneness. My reaction to that was: "Four years?! If he'd had a guide or a mentor, he could've done it *so* much faster."

Essentially, what this monk took 4 years to learn is exactly what I'm teaching you to do in this book. My private coaching clients learn these steps in even greater detail and are able to implement them in roughly a quarter of the time it took for the monk to do the same thing all alone! But if you *do* decide to go it alone, aren't getting the results you want, and are feeling frustrated, just remember that it took that monk four years of solitude to do this same thing when he was going it alone, as well.

Don't feel sad, guilty, or depressed if things are not going as well as you hoped, because that's also a test. You are standing at the patience pole here; you have to be committed to your outcome in order to make it through. Don't flip yourself over and tie yourself up in knots. Just be diligent, do the work, and be patient. Take small steps. They may not be perfect, you may falter, and some days even feel like a failure, but as long as you stay committed to your goal, you will achieve results. You will be able to look back and recognize a change in yourself because you are powerful!

You have so much potential locked away within you, but it has been pushed down and lain dormant for so long that you don't know how to use your power any longer. It is STILL there. You just have to choose to find it, resurrect it, and use it.

No matter what obstacles you encounter, you can rise above them and feel your way forward using the techniques and lessons in this book. But if at any time you feel stuck, lost, or in need of more help, I urge you to please reach out to me. I don't want you to flounder around, caught in a storm of self-doubt, and feeling unable to move forward.

Change is never easy. That is the most important thing to remember. It's NOT easy, so don't waste your time trying to find ways to make it easier. Don't think there's got to be an easier way to do this. You can be the monk and spend 4 years in "retreat" on an island, or you can spend significantly less time using the techniques in this book or working with me directly.

I have always found that I get where I want to be faster and more efficiently when I work with someone supportive. Without help, I still accomplish my goals, but it takes me years compared to months. Remember that monk? I don't know about you, but I'd rather move forward in months rather than waiting years.

So, remember, obstacles can come from anywhere, in any form, and their goal is to test you, to see if you'll get thrown off your path. If that happens, and you get derailed and lost, you can always find your way back using the CONNECTING program, or you can work with someone to make sure that you meet your goal.

So do your best not to get derailed, and recognize when an obstacle is thrown in your path. If you are finding unsupportive people around you that are creating a toxic environment, move away from them, end those friendships, or just spend time building more positive relationships in your life to balance out that negativity. You are who you surround yourself with. Make sure those around you are spiritual superstars full of love, positivity and support. Allow your magic to shine and those souls who are confident, loving and supportive will be there to love you along the journey.

Remember, your goal is to ride the happy
trails again, not walk them all alone.

Wisdom from Paris

*My equine friends who are living on the
plains in freedom encounter obstacles
every day. Where do they find water, food
or shelter? How do they escape predators?
Where is it safe to rest so that the mares
can foal? How long should they stay in one
place?*

*If they were to give up there would be no
more wild horses. You are a wild horse,
too. Don't give up.*

You can contact me, and find more information
about *Ride Free* or about
Equine-Facilitated Learning at:

www.dreamwest.co

About The Author

Miranda K. Velasquez is a marriage and family therapist trainee and spiritual life coach with a huge passion and love for horses. She has been a horse owner for more than 15 years and she recognizes and connects with the deep spirituality of the horse.

She is on a mission to help others create a strong and meaningful bond with their own horses, to look deeper within themselves, and find the connection between their soul, and the ancient ways of the horse.

Miranda is also a healer, assisting both animals and humans along their healing journey. She has degrees in Veterinary Technology, Middle Eastern Studies and Religion, and is currently working on her licensure for Marriage and Family Therapy.

She is certified by The HERD Institute in Equine-Facilitated Learning and conducts healing and experiential sessions in person.

You can find out more at www.dreamwest.co.

Made in the USA
Las Vegas, NV
14 April 2022